# THE LANGUAGE OF VICTORY

# THE LANGUAGE OF VICTORY

## VICTORY

*American Indian Code Talkers of World War I and World War II*

GARY ROBINSON

# The Language of Victory
## American Indian Code Talkers of World War I and World War II

Look for the companion
*The Language of Victory* DVD,
which features never-before-seen
interviews with Choctaw, Comanche,
and Navajo code talkers
of World War II.

The Cover Art

The original cover art by American Indian artist Michael Horse
was created especially for this project in the historic art form
known as the Plains Indian Ledger Style, which came into being
in the late 1800s when a few American Indians captured by
the cavalry created scenes on ledger paper while imprisoned.
The background of the cover is the schematic rendering of a
World War II field radio used by many code talkers. For more
on the art of Michael Horse go to www.michaelhorse.com

A portion of the
sales of this book and the accompanying DVD
goes to the nonprofit
National American Indian Veterans
to support programs and services
benefiting American Indian veterans.
For more information, go to www.naivonline.org.

## Other Works by the Author

*Tribal Sovereignty: The Right to Self-Rule* (educational DVD), Tribal Eye Productions, Santa Ynez, CA, 2007.

*From Warriors to Soldiers: The History of American Indian Service in the United States Military* (nonfiction book), by Gary Robinson and Phil Lucas, iUniverse, Bloomington, IL, 2008.

*I Am the Warrior* (educational DVD), Tribal Eye Productions, 2009.

*Tribal Journeys of the Pacific Northwest* (educational DVD), Tribal Eye Productions, Santa Ynez, CA 2009.

*Native American Night Before Christmas* (children's book), Clearlight Publishers, Santa Fe, NM, 2010, www.clearlightbooks.com.

*Native American Twelve Days of Christmas* (children's book), Clearlight Publishers, Santa Fe, NM, 2011, www.clearlightbooks.com.

Short original videos by the author, and excerpts of longer videos, may be viewed on the Tribal Eye Productions' YouTube Channel at www.youtube.com/tribaleyepro.

*For more information or to order any these items, contact:*

Tribal Eye Productions
PO Box 1123
Santa Ynez, CA 93460
Ph: 805-245-9630
Email: garyd1123@gmail.com

# Contents

# Foreword

Since America's beginning, whenever the call of duty has come, indigenous American peoples have stepped forward to proudly defend and serve the United States in both peacetime and in war. Yet, outside their own local communities, many American Indian veterans have not received the recognition they deeply deserve nor, in many cases, have they obtained all the benefits and services they rightfully earned.

This book, *The Language of Victory*, is another chapter in the ongoing story of unique contributions made to the democracy, freedom, and cultural diversity of America. And as revealed in these pages, it provides another example of delayed or overlooked recognition experienced by American Indian veterans.

For far too long, American Indian warriors have been this nation's forgotten veterans. Important issues that affect indigenous American veterans include a lack of adequate housing and the inability to receive proper representation to obtain health care, earned compensation, pension, and burial benefits for their families.

Historically, American Indians have served in the armed forces at the highest rate of any ethnic group in the United States, and Indian people have a proud legacy of defending our homeland. These facts must be acknowledged by national Veterans Affairs policies and translated into actions that support our people.

There has long been the need for one effective, representative body that speaks for the American Indian, Alaska Native, Native Samoan, and Native Hawaiian veteran. That's why the nonprofit

National American Indian Veterans organization, or NAIV, was created.

NAIV is devoted to representing and supporting American Indian and other indigenous veterans and advocating for the improvement of their quality of life, and that of their families. It is the heart, soul, and voice of the indigenous American veteran.

The United States Department of Veteran Affairs recognizes NAIV as the one national organization to represent the unique needs, concerns, and issues of indigenous veterans to Congress and the Veterans Administration. NAIV has also been recognized as the voice of the American Indian veteran by the National Congress of American Indians (NCAI) as well as the National Association of State Directors of Veteran's Affairs (NASDVA).

Our federal charter was introduced in the 108th Congress and, as of this printing, is currently pending approval in the House Judiciary Committee as House Bill HR933. This bill is important to American Indian veterans in gaining full recognition of their needs and concerns.

As National Commander of NAIV, I invite you to increase your knowledge and awareness of the important part played by American Indians in the history of our great nation. I also invite you to join us in making a positive difference in the lives of American Indian veterans and their families. To find out how, go to our website at www.naivonline.org or call our national headquarters at 1-225-686-7627.

Thank you.

*Don Loudner (Sioux)*
*National Commander*
*National American Indian Veterans, Inc.*

# Introduction

By now almost everyone in the United States has heard of the Navajo code talkers of World War II. Several books have been written on the subject, multiple documentary films have been produced, and Hollywood even made a movie about them (*Windtalkers*, 2002, starring Adam Beach). So much attention has been given to the Navajo code talkers that one might think they were the *only* code talkers.

But a growing number of Americans have begun to hear about the "other" code talkers, such as the *originals:* the Choctaw code talkers of World War I. Several magazine and newspaper articles, at least one book, and a PBS documentary have told their story.

But few people outside American Indian communities know that, according to various sources, at least *twenty* American Indian languages were used to send secret US military messages during World War I and World War II—messages that were never decoded by the enemy.

Time after time, during both world wars, American military commanders credited our nation's military victories, in part, to the unerring delivery of coded messages sent and received by American Indian soldiers fluent in their own tribal languages—languages thought to have been obsolete before that time, languages that many natives had been punished for speaking in government-run boarding schools.

In 2008, Congress passed the Code Talker Recognition Act designed to bring recognition and honor for, in the words of the act, "the dedication and valor of Native American (*American*

*Indian*) code talkers." Sioux army veteran and NAIV Commander Don Loudner was part of a group instrumental in getting that legislation passed. The group included Chief Gregory Pyle of the Choctaw Nation of Oklahoma; Judy Allen, public relations director for the Choctaw Nation; Wallace Coffey, the former chairman of the Comanche Nation; Lanny Aseperme, councilman and veteran from the Comanche Nation; and Andrea Page, a Sioux college instructor living in New York at the time.

This book explores the history of military communications and the unique place that American Indian code talkers, and their languages, have in that history and the history of America. The text includes never-before-published interviews with a few Comanche, Navajo, and Choctaw code talkers, most of whom are now, unfortunately deceased. This project also documents the long-overdue recognition and honor that finally came to be bestowed on the multi-tribal code talkers, including the creation of the Congressional medals awarded to the tribes and individuals whose languages were used as military codes.

Finally we'll reflect on what might have been lost if tribal languages had died, if tenacious native peoples hadn't struggled to preserve and pass on their spoken words, which became the weapons of war spoken in the *language of victory.*

One final introductory note: NAIV has officially adopted the use of the term "American Indian" instead of "Native American" when referring to America's indigenous people. They do so because technically any person born in the United States is a native American, just as any person born a Texan is called a native Texan. NAIV believes that the term "American Indian" more accurately reflects the historical term that a majority of indigenous peoples themselves prefer and accept. In deference to and respect for the National American Indian Veterans organization, this author uses "American Indian" in the pages of this book except when quoting other speakers or federal legislation.

# CHAPTER ONE

# Military Communications: An Overview

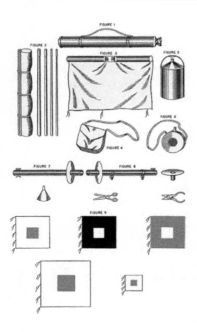

*Early US Army Signal Corps field kit with flags for signaling.*

*US Army Signal Corps code class – WWII era*

Communicating effectively has always been an important part of waging war and keeping the peace. Military commanders must be able to communicate orders to their units in the field to execute their strategies and win battles, and reports must be sent from the battlefront back to headquarters so that commanders know if their strategies are working.

Over the centuries, as armies grew larger and more complex and the distances between headquarters and the frontlines increased, it became more and more difficult to orchestrate various military components into one successful operation. Thus separate communications units developed to handle the complexities of military communications. And, of course, an extremely necessary component of these communications is secrecy—the enemy must not be able to find out what your plans are—where and how and when you're going to strike. Secrecy and surprise are key elements when it comes to winning victories.

As long as military units remained relatively small and engaged in close hand-to-hand combat, a commander's booming voice provided an effective means for transmitting orders on the battlefield. Armies also successfully used musical instruments, such as trumpets and bugles, as signaling devices. But for long-distance communications, ancient commanders often relied on runners or mounted messengers.

The use of messengers for delivering all kinds of messages developed in most societies in ancient times, and, in some cases, this method still constitutes a valuable means of direct communication to an intended receiver over long distances.

Legend has it that in 490 BC a Greek runner delivered to Athens the news of Greece's victory over the Persians at a place called Marathon, and then the runner died from the exertion. This heroic feat is said to have given rise to the athletic event known as the marathon.

Later, military leaders such as Alexander the Great, Hannibal, and Caesar developed elaborate systems of relays by which messages were carried from one messenger post to another by messengers mounted on horseback and traveling at top speed. In that way, they were able to maintain contact with their homelands during far-off military campaigns and to transmit messages with adequate speed.

At the close of the twelfth century, the Mongolian warlord Genghis Khan not only established an extensive system of messenger posts from Europe to his Mongol capital, but he also made use of homing pigeons as messengers. As his military victories grew and the lands falling under his command stretched, he established pigeon relay posts across Asia and much of eastern Europe. Because he was both political and military ruler of his domains, it was necessary for him to send kingly orders to all sectors of his kingdom, and he effectively used both human and fowl messengers to transmit instructions to his subordinates.

Many American Indian societies used foot messengers to communicate not only military messages but other types of important social messages as well. A prime example of the effective use of the "Indian runner" was during the Pueblo Revolt of 1680, in which the American Indians of New Mexico threw off the oppressive yoke of Spanish rule. Popé, the spiritual and military mastermind of the revolt, prepared a set of knotted ropes for each of his runners to carry to the far-flung pueblo villages strewn up and down the Rio Grande. Each knot on the cord represented a day's count until the fateful day of revolution, when all of the Pueblos would rise up against the hated outsiders. And rise up they did, expelling the Spaniards from their midst, but unfortunately for the pueblos it was not for good.

Of course, the process of delivering messages on foot is comparatively slow and is really only effective when the distances are not too far.

American Indians used several other means of communications for warfare and hunting that proved both appropriate and successful within their natural lifestyles. Certain animal calls signaled that warriors were in place and ready for attack. Smoke signals might represent the call of danger or the return to safety and peace. Drums were sometimes used to summon warriors or neighboring camps. Charcoal and ochre markings in prearranged locations could indicate the location of game or an enemy. Trail signs made of stacked stones or tree cuts could indicate the direction for hunters or warriors to follow or the direction to avoid. Tribes of the Plains, who spoke different languages, developed a system of intertribal sign language made up of arm and hand gestures that allowed for the effective exchange of information.

Back in Europe near the end of the eighteenth century, the French engineer Claude Chappe developed a system of communication that employed towers or poles with movable arms near the top. The raising or lowering of the arms in the proper combinations indicated specific letters, words, or phrases. Using this system, messages could be sent over long distances in hours rather than days. In the early 1800s, visual telegraph duties, known as semaphores, were assigned to units of engineer troops. Various forms of these "optical telegraphs" were developed and used by different European nations.

At the same time that these elementary methods of signal communication were being evolved on land, a comparable development was going on at sea. Early signaling between naval vessels was by prearranged messages transmitted by flags, lights, or the movement of a sail.

The idea of using coded messages came into use in Europe in the sixteenth century. Many codes were based simply on the number and position of signal flags or lights or on a number of cannon shots. In the seventeenth century, British admirals and ship commanders developed regular codes for naval communication, and, near the end of the eighteenth century, British Admiral Richard Kempenfelt devised a plan of flag signaling similar to the one still in use today. Of course, these methods have been refined and improved through the decades.

In the United States, various branches of our fledgling country's military came into being through acts of Congress in the 1780s. And each branch of service put to use the best in existing means of military communications.

However the most significant development of signal communication for wartime use came after the invention of the electric telegraph by Samuel F. B. Morse. He successfully demonstrated electric communication between Washington, DC, and Baltimore in 1844, and immediately provided a completely new means of rapid signal communication. His Morse code, in which letters of the alphabet are communicated through a series of dots and dashes, used an electric key and sounder. This new technology was soon put to military use to supplement the various means of visual signaling.

In the United States, the new device saw limited service during the war against Mexico (1846–1848) because it still had a few bugs and was disastrously unreliable. So the army only used the telegraph to communicate from its Washington office to offices in Baltimore, Philadelphia, and New York. As a precautionary measure, however, each telegraphed message was followed up with a letter.

In 1867, the British navy adopted a system of "flash signaling," which was developed by a member of its high command. This was essentially an adaptation of the Morse code to lights. But the first actual application of the telegraph in time of war was made by the British in 1854 during the Crimean War. However its capabilities were not well understood, and therefore it was not widely used. Three years later, the Brits made full use of the telegraph in the Indian Mutiny of 1857, and its use was a deciding factor in victory.

The United States Army became the first army in the world to create a separate communications unit, beginning with the appointment in 1860 of a signal officer to the War Department's army staff. This event marked the official beginning of the US Army Signal Corps. The flag-signaling system then put to use had been developed by an assistant army surgeon, Albert J. Myer, who had previously worked both as a civilian telegraph operator and an aid to the deaf. Combining these two experiences, he came up with the signaling system that became the army signal corps' first wartime signaling system. Myer was named the first signal officer and given the rank of major.

Ironically, the first use of Myer's signaling system in the field was against the Navajos in October of 1860. Myer and his men accompanied troops on the campaign, maintaining communication between the columns, performing reconnaissance, and reporting by signals. The simplicity of the system, with its lightweight, portable equipment, made it well suited to use in the rugged terrain of the southwest.

When the opening shots of the Civil War were fired the following spring at Fort Sumter, South Carolina, the newly formed army signal corps was called into action. Myer became its first instructor and operations supervisor.

As military signaling became more routine and systematic within the armed forces, signal security started to become a serious problem: enemy forces could learn the meanings of the messages that were being sent and therefore anticipate the coming action. During the Civil War, the chief of staff of the Army of the Potomac expressed this very concern during an important battle when he ordered that signals not be used because the enemy could read them. The chief signal officer at the time complained in his report of the battle that ""the corps is distrusted, and considered unsafe as a means of transmitting important messages. It is well known that the enemy can read our signals when the regular code is used."

To prevent Confederate forces from reading Union messages, the signal corps developed mechanized means of creating codes that could be changed on a regular basis, therefore making it next to impossible for an enemy to break the code. This became a regularly used technique that extended well into WWII. Both senders and receivers would be given a new code clue that would allow them to adjust their "cipher wheels" to find the matching code. As long as both ends of the transmission were on the same place on the wheel, coded messages could be sent without enemy translation.

Near the close of the nineteenth century, the wireless telegraph, or radio, made its appearance, and military leaders the world over quickly saw its potential for military and naval signaling. Development was rapid, and by 1914 the new technology had been adopted and put to extensive use by the armies and navies of the world. With such widespread application, it soon became obvious that wireless telegraphy had its flaws when it came to military messaging: it lacked secrecy because messages could be easily heard by ally and enemy alike. This led to the further development of extensive and complicated codes and ciphers as a necessary part of military signaling. And a new battlefield of the airwaves arose, pitting the cryptographer against the cryptanalyst on each side of any international conflict. A nation's ability to create an unbreakable communication code for wartime use became *the* ultimate challenge.

With the need for rapidly developed technical improvements to radio communications for wartime applications, American resources in the military, scientific, and industrial fields joined forces to create better and more reliable means of transmitting messages during battle. Dramatic technical developments during and after WWI made it possible for signal corps personnel to consistently communicate vital messages that saved lives and won wars. But throughout all the technical advances in communications, it has always been the American soldier who has brought the courage, determination, and ingenuity necessary to make the equipment work under fire.

# CHAPTER TWO

# Tribes and Tribal Languages before World War I

| | | | | | | | |
|---|---|---|---|---|---|---|---|
| Ꭰ | a | Ꭶ | ga | Ꭷ | ka | Ꭽ | ha |
| Ꮃ | la | Ꮉ | ma | Ꮎ | na | Ꮏ | hna |
| Ꮐ | nah | Ꮖ | qua | Ꮜ | sa | Ꮝ | s |
| Ꮣ | da | Ꮤ | ta | Ꮬ | dla | Ꮭ | tla |
| Ꮳ | tsa | Ꮹ | wa | Ꮿ | ya | Ꭱ | e |
| Ꭸ | ge | Ꭾ | he | Ꮄ | le | Ꮊ | me |
| Ꮑ | ne | Ꮗ | que | Ꮞ | se | Ꮥ | de |
| Ꮦ | te | Ꮮ | tle | Ꮴ | tse | Ꮺ | we |
| Ᏸ | ye | Ꭲ | i | Ꭹ | gi | Ꭿ | hi |
| Ꮅ | li | Ꮋ | mi | Ꮒ | ni | Ꮘ | qui |
| Ꮟ | si | Ꮧ | di | Ꮨ | ti | Ꮯ | tli |
| Ꮵ | tsi | Ꮻ | wi | Ᏹ | yi | Ꭳ | o |
| Ꭺ | go | Ꮀ | ho | Ꮆ | lo | Ꮌ | mo |
| Ꮓ | no | Ꮙ | quo | Ꮠ | so | Ꮩ | do |
| Ꮰ | tlo | Ꮶ | tso | Ꮼ | wo | Ᏺ | yo |
| Ꭴ | u | Ꭻ | gu | Ꮁ | hu | Ꮇ | lu |
| Ꮍ | mu | Ꮔ | nu | Ꮚ | quu | Ꮡ | su |
| Ꮪ | du | Ꮱ | tlu | Ꮷ | tsu | Ꮽ | wu |
| Ᏻ | yu | Ꭵ | v | Ꭼ | gv | Ꮂ | hv |
| Ꮈ | lv | Ꮕ | nv | Ꮛ | quv | | |
| Ꮢ | sv | Ꮫ | dv | Ꮲ | tlv | | |
| Ꮸ | tsv | Ꮾ | wv | Ᏼ | yv | | |

*A Cherokee alphabet, using unique characters, was created by a Cherokee man named Sequoyah in the 1820s and was one of the very few early attempts to create a written version of an American Indian language.*

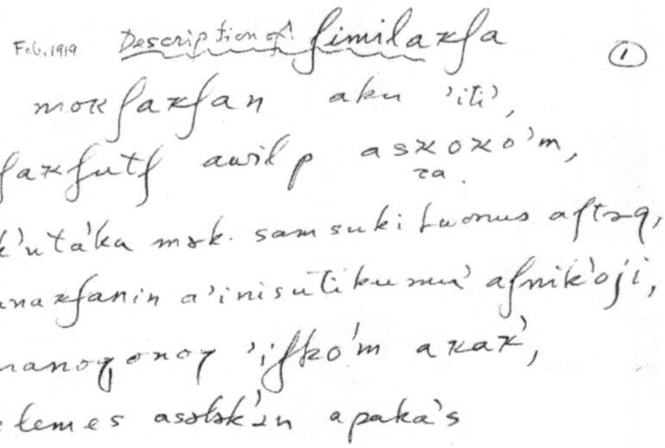

*This is a portion of one of the hundreds of thousands of pages of notes left by the anthropologist and linguist John P. Harrington who meticulously recorded many disappearing American Indian languages in the early 1900s.*

As any fourth grade student knows, American Indian tribes have lived on the North American continent for thousands of years and have fought to defend their homelands, families, resources, and ways of life from all outside threats, including European immigrants, American pioneers, and the United States military.

Many tribes had well-developed warrior traditions that were more complex and contained more mental and spiritual depth than anything depicted in Hollywood westerns, and American history books are filled with the names of native warriors who put their lives on the line in defense of their people.

US military leaders from George Washington to Andrew Jackson and Teddy Roosevelt recognized the unique abilities of American Indian warriors to win battles using unconventional means with almost supernatural force, and they put those skills to successful use time and time again. (See the author's nonfiction book *From Warriors to Soldiers* to explore tribal warrior traditions and the history of American Indians in the military in more detail.)

One of the things native people fought for, and continue to fight for, is their identity and the right to maintain that identity. Language is a central and defining element of anyone's culture and personal identity. Contained within a language are a people's view of the world, their sense of place within it, and their relationship to it. Destroy a nation's language and you also destroy its connection to its own past and future.

People's ways of living, their histories, and their philosophies are all understood and communicated through language. Although most American Indians now speak English to some degree, many still consider their traditional languages to be very important. During the past one hundred years, many tribal languages have been lost or are now in danger of being lost. When the last speaker of a language passes away, that language becomes extinct, and therefore American Indian communities are working hard to keep their native languages alive.

As the United States strengthened its independence from European nations and grasped for larger pieces of the American continent, the nation's treatment of indigenous peoples fluctuated with the policies of annihilation, relocation, and assimilation. In the

1700s and 1800s, many tribes were forced off their lands and confined to reservations where they endured hardships that included racism, poverty, and efforts to eradicate their traditional cultures. Some of these efforts were part of a movement to *"Americanize"* the Indian.

The Indian Removal Act of 1830, which called for the relocation of tribes living east of the Mississippi River to lands west of the river, reflected the government's goal of removing Indians who were seen as impeding American expansion. While the law did not authorize the forced removal of tribal peoples, it authorized the president to negotiate land exchange treaties with tribes located in the eastern regions. A follow-up law, the Intercourse Law of 1834, prohibited US citizens from entering tribal lands granted by any such treaties without permission, though it was often ignored.

Though the Indian Removal Act made the relocation of the tribes voluntary, it was often abused by government officials, including President Andrew Jackson. One infamous example of this abuse is the Treaty of New Echota of 1835, negotiated and signed by a small faction of Cherokee tribal members—not the tribal leadership. It resulted in the forced relocation of the tribe in 1838, during Andrew Jackson's administration, in which an estimated four thousand Cherokees died in the march from their traditional homelands in the Carolinas to the recently created Indian Territory. This march became known as the Trail of Tears.

But in the decades that followed, white settlers encroached heavily into these western lands that had been set aside for tribes. American settlers eventually made homesteads from coast to coast, leaving no tribe untouched by the Americanizing influence of white traders, farmers, and soldiers.

In his State of the Union Address in December of 1871, Ulysses Grant stated that "many tribes of Indians have been induced to settle upon reservations, to cultivate the soil, to perform productive labor of various kinds, and to partially accept civilization. They are being cared for in such a way, it is hoped, as to induce those still pursuing their old habits of life to embrace the only opportunity which is left them to avoid extermination." The prevailing view toward the American Indian at the time is evident in Grant's statement: change or die.

In the 1890s, as the United States continued to expand, tribal lands were once again confiscated and reduced further in size to make way for more white settlers. In 1889, Congress authorized the opening for homestead settlement of tribal lands seized from the Indian Territory.

Languages were particularly targeted in the US government's efforts to assimilate American Indians into the mainstream. The centerpiece of these efforts was the network of Indian Boarding Schools established in the late 1800s by the US government and various churches in different regions of the county. American Indian children were forcibly removed from their home communities and sent to these schools where they were forbidden to speak their own languages and punished if they did. The stated objective of these schools, according to Lieutenant Colonel R.H. Pratt, architect of the system, was to "kill the Indian, but save the man." Unfortunately, nearly half of those subjected to the boarding school experience did not survive that experience.

In the boarding school strategy, the assault on a native child's tribal culture was complete. These children were forced to cut their hair and replace their traditional clothing with uniforms. They also had to replace their indigenous names, steeped in rich cultural traditions, with meaningless English ones.

They were taught that their cultures were inferior, and their own ancient religious practices were replaced with a rigid form of Christianity. Teachers were encouraged to use ridicule and humiliation to teach native youth to be ashamed of their "Indianness."

Boarding schools had a long-term negative effect on the self-esteem of Indian students and on possible continuation of native languages and cultures.

In spite of these culturally destructive behaviors and beliefs, American Indian students did also manage to acquire knowledge of the workings of the white man's world and to learn skills that in some cases proved to be helpful later in life. One area that proved useful was, for those who joined the military, a regimented lifestyle because the boarding school curriculum usually included some of the skills necessary for life in the military.

During the opening years of the twentieth century, mainstream white America continued its national debate concerning the fate of American Indians. The "assimilationists," as they were known then, believed that Indians should continue to be mainstreamed in all aspects of life including clothing, customs, hairstyles, housing, employment, religion, and education.

"Separatists" tended to believe that Indians were incapable of full integration into American society due to their inferior nature, a belief that continued to be applied to African-Americans as well.

American Indians, it seems, were seldom consulted regarding these issues. Many were eager to prove themselves within the national arena in all walks of life while firmly maintaining their preference for practicing traditional native ways. To indigenous people, the two are not mutually exclusive.

With America's entry into World War I in 1917, several Indian tribes declared war on Germany independently of the United States. Thousands of American Indian men and women volunteered for military service but were rejected because they did not speak or read English.

Simultaneously, many US military leaders were still opposed to using Indians in regular service and needed convincing otherwise. Several prominent citizens with close ties to Congressional leaders finally paved the way for Indian participation in military service.

At the time, the Department of the Interior still operated about twenty-five boarding schools, and those automatically became recruiting stations. At Virginia's Hampton Institute, one Lakota student, Charles Roy Morsea, gave a patriotic speech to his fellow students encouraging their enlistment. He explained that his father had served earlier in the Spanish-American War and was already fighting in France with General Pershing.

Despite a variety of barriers, more than seventeen thousand Indians saw active service in the army and navy during the First World War. Some two-thirds were volunteers, even though Indians weren't allowed to be citizens on a national scale until 1924 with passage of the Indian Citizenship Act.

Why did so many American Indian men enlist? Partly because tribal societies still regarded their warriors with the utmost respect.

Native men had trained at a young age to develop the spiritual, mental, emotional, and physical strength needed to become warriors. Many tribes continued their warrior societies with their own ceremonies, songs, dances, and regalia. But they no longer had any means of achieving warrior status. So many turned to military service as a way of achieving that honored status.

# CHAPTER THREE

# World War I and the Birth of American Indian "Code Talkers"

*World War I field telephone.*

*The first: Choctaw code talkers of
World War I.*

As mentioned in the previous chapter, at the onset of America's participation in World War I in 1917 American Indians were not citizens of the United States, and, to most Americans, the languages they spoke were considered obsolete. Little did anyone know that a few of these so-called obsolete languages, spoken by soldiers who weren't American citizens, would help turn the tide and win what became known as the Great War.

To the surprise of many of US commanding officers, American Indian soldiers proved to be adept at learning to use complex equipment and speak other languages. However, their methods, as noted before, were not always orthodox.

For example, two Comanche soldiers from a unit endangered by not knowing the German strategy waited till nightfall, stripped down, and covered their bodies completely in whitewash. They crept out into No Man's Land (the zone between opposing enemy trenches) and waited by the enemy lines until daylight. There they stood, absolutely still, blending in with a collection of wooden posts, overhearing the enemy communications.

Personal accounts of American Indian heroism were numerous, and the contributions made by American Indian soldiers were noticed by British and French commanders. Ferdinand Foch, marshal of France, wrote, "I cannot forget the brilliant service which the valorous Indian soldiers of the American army have rendered to the common cause, and the energy, as well as the courage, which they have shown to bring about victory ..."

According to native soldiers, the use of tribal languages as codes did not arise from a brilliant strategic military plan devised by army headquarters but rather from desperate need on the field of combat. The Germans had become masters at listening in and decoding all US Army field communications in Europe. Every planned battle and maneuver was effectively thwarted by German artillery, air, and ground troops. They obviously knew what was coming, and America was losing the war.

Though reports from army personnel give non-Indian military leaders the credit for the idea, it was Indian soldiers themselves who presented the idea of using one of their languages as a code. Having exhausted every other means of transmitting coded information, US commanders believed it was worth a try.

Initially a group of eight Choctaws was trained in setting up and using the field telephone. Since there were no specific Choctaw words for many of the military terms they needed to communicate, many existing Choctaw words were substituted. For example, the first, second, and third battalions were called One Grain of Corn, Two Grains of Corn, and Three Grains of Corn respectively. The term adopted for machine gun was "little gun shoot fast." Thus an entire coded military vocabulary was developed.

When it came time to test the system, one Choctaw was placed at each of the allied field camps to send and receive messages in the tribal language. The messages were then translated into English.

The remarkable results of this experiment were reported by Colonel A. W. Bloor, commander of the 142nd Infantry Division operating in France, in his memo to the headquarters of the American Expeditionary Forces.

*Date: January 23, 1919, A.P.O. No. 796*
*From: C.O. 142nd Infantry*
*To: The Commanding General 36th Division (Attention Capt. Spence)*
*Headquarters - 142nd Infantry, A.E.F.(Allied Expeditionary Forces)*
*Subject: Transmitting messages in Choctaw*

*In compliance with memorandum, Headquarters 36th Division, January 21, 1919, to C.O. 142nd Infantry, the following account is submitted. In the first action of the 142nd Infantry at St. Etienne, it was recognized that of all the various methods of liaison the telephone presented the greatest possibilities. The field of rocket signals is restricted to a small number of agreed signals. The runner system is slow and hazardous. T. P. S. (Telegraphic Signaling) is always an uncertain quantity. It may work beautifully and again, it may be entirely worthless. The available means, therefore, for the rapid and full transmission of information are the radio, buzzer and telephone, and of these the telephone was by far the superior, provided it could be used without hindrance, provided straight to the point information could be given.*

It was well understood however, that the German was a past master of "listening in." Moreover, from St. Etienne to the Aisne we had traveled through a county netted with German wire and cables. We established PCs (Permanent Commands) in dugouts and houses, but recently occupied by him. There was every reason to believe every decipherable message or word going over our wires also went to the enemy. A rumor was out that our Division had given false coordinates of our supply dump, and that in thirty minutes the enemy shells were falling on the point. We felt sure the enemy knew too much. It was therefore necessary to code every message of importance and coding and decoding took valuable time.

While comparatively inactive at Vaux-Champagne, it was remembered that the regiment possessed a company of Indians. They spoke twenty-six different language or dialects, only four or five of which were ever written. There was hardly one chance in a million that Fritz would be able to translate these dialects and the plan to have these Indians transmit telephone messages was adopted. The regiment was fortunate in having two Indian officers who spoke several of the dialects. Indians from the Choctaw tribe were chosen and one placed in each P.C. (*Note: while this commander claims the idea came from within the Army's intelligence unit, several of the Choctaw soldiers claimed the idea was there's.)

The first use of the Indians was made in ordering a delicate withdrawal of two companies of the 2nd En. from Chufilly to Chardoney on the night of October 26th. This movement was completed without mishap ... The Indians were used repeatedly on the 27th in preparation for the assault on Forest Farm. The enemy's complete surprise is evidence that he could not decipher the messages.

After the withdrawal of the regiment to Louppy-le-Petit, a number of Indians were detailed for training in transmitting messages over the telephone. The instruction was carried on by the Liaison Officer Lieutenant Black. It had been found that the Indian's vocabulary of military terms was insufficient. The Indian (word) for "Big Gun" was used to indicate artillery. "Little gun shoot fast" was substituted for machine gun and the battalions were indicated by one, two and three grains of corn. It was found that the Indian tongues do not permit verbatim translation, but at the end of the short training period at

*Louppy-le-Petit, the results were very gratifying and it is believed, had the regiment gone back into the line, fine results would have been obtained. We were confident the possibilities of the telephone had been obtained without its hazards.*

*A. W. Bloor, Colonel*
*142nd Infantry*
*Commanding*

According to research done by the Department of Defense, there were possibly twenty-three American Indian soldiers from different tribes who used their tribal languages to send and receive coded messages during World War I. Most of them were Choctaws, as the Choctaw language was most extensively used. However, the Comanche and Cherokee languages are also reported to have been used.

It's unfortunate that a respected history of the army's signal corps, published by the US Army Center of Military History, makes no mention of the American Indian code talkers' contribution during World War I.

As they proved successful in using their native language as a code, more Choctaws were quickly pressed into service, expanding the original eight to at least eighteen. Choctaw tribal documents list these names on their World War I Choctaw code talkers list: Tobias Frazier, Victor Brown, Joseph Oklahombi, Otis Leader, Ben Hampton, Albert Billy, Walter Veach, Ben Carterby, James Edwards, Solomon Louis, Peter Maytubby, Mitchell Bobb, Calvin Wilson, Jeff Nelson, Joseph Davenport, George Davenport, Noel Johnson, and Robert Taylor. These men were members of the army's Thirty-Sixth Division.

Later, a captured German officer confessed that his intelligence personnel "were completely confused by the Indian language and gained no benefit whatsoever from their wiretaps." Up until the time American Indian languages were spoken over military telephone lines, the Germans had successfully deciphered coded messages because most Americans were of European origin and their sense of language, coded or otherwise, came from the languages of that continent. Consequently, Germans had a good idea of the different ways Americans might try to render English into codes. American

Indian languages are not based on European tongues, so Germans had no reference when attempting to translate and decode native code.

"Within 24 hours after the Choctaw language was pressed into service, the tide of the battle had turned and in less than 72 hours the Allies were on full attack," Commander Bloor reported.

Of course, the tribes are very proud of the story of the original code talkers of World War I. The Choctaws of Oklahoma erected a granite monument at the entrance to their capitol grounds that bears the engraved names of the men who used the language to help win World War I. Toward the end of the war, Cherokee, Comanche, Cheyenne, and Osage tribal members from Oklahoma also served as code talkers, according to Department of Defense documents.

It should be noted that the term "code talker" was not coined until World War II or shortly after. The World War I code talkers never referred to themselves this way nor did anyone else. It seems that these soldiers usually referred to their activity as merely "talking on the radio," by which they meant the field telephone.

# CHAPTER FOUR

# World War II: Code Talking Perfected

*Comanche code talker trainees of World War II.*

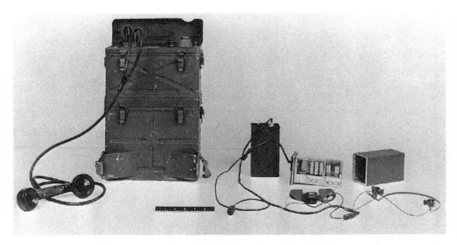

*World War II US Army backpack radio telephone gear.*

Before the outbreak of World War II, Adolf Hitler sent an undercover team of German anthropologists to the United States in an attempt to learn American Indian languages because he'd learned of the successful use of American Indian code talkers during World War I. However, it proved an overwhelming task for the Germans to learn the many tribal languages and dialects that existed.

Because of these Nazi anthropologists' attempts to learn tribal languages, the US Army did not implement a large-scale code talker program for the European Theater of the Second World War. However, anticipating that the United States might be drawn into the expanding war, the director of the Fort Cobb Indian Conservation Corps camp of Oklahoma, a Comanche named William Karty, proposed that the army begin using the Comanche language for coded communications. Karty's suggestion fell on receptive ears, and he was authorized to recruit volunteers for this special mission. The primary requirement was the ability to speak and understand English and Comanche fluently.

Comanche code talker Roderick Red Elk explains what happened. "There was a man that came down and talked to several of us for the purpose of joining the army to become code talkers. This was December, 1940. I got sworn in January 1, 1941."

So, in December 1940, the army did recruit seventeen Comanches to become code talkers. These were Charles Chibitty, Haddon Codynah, Robert Holder, Forrest Kassanavoid, Wellington Mihecoby, Perry Noyabad, Clifford Otitivo, Simmons Parker, Melvin Permansu, Elgin Red Elk, Roderick Red Elk, Albert Nahquaddy Jr., Larry Saupitty, Morris Tabbyetchy (Sunrise), Anthony Tabbytite, Ralph Wahnee, and Willie Yacheschi.

After graduating from West Point in 1941, Lieutenant Hugh F. Foster joined the army signal corps and was sent to Fort Benning, Georgia, where he was put in charge of training the Comanches who'd been recruited for code talking.

Assigned to the Fourth Infantry Division's Fourth Signal Company at Fort Benning, they received basic training, which was followed by phone, radio, Morse code, and semaphore training. These were the only American Indian soldiers who were officially trained to become code talkers for deployment in Europe.

Red Elk continues describing their experience: "After basic training, they started us on the different types of communications, how to operate, tear down, and repair the telephone, the radio ..."

Most of these recruits had attended Indian boarding schools where they had become accustomed to military-style discipline and been punished for speaking their native tongue. Their mastery of military skills amazed the army drill sergeant assigned to train them.

By October 30, 1941, the Comanches had completed their training and were conducting field exercises soon thereafter.

Comanches of the Fourth Signal Company compiled a vocabulary of over one hundred code terms using words or phrases in their own language.

Red Elk said that in the army there are "a lot of military terms with no Comanche word for them, so we had to sit down and figure out a name for each, for instance, like 'gun.'

"We had just one name for 'gun'—(he says the Comanche word)—which means 'gun.' In the military you have all types of guns. You got your artillery, you got your small arms, you got your machine guns, the different caliber machine guns. And we had to work out a word for each of those." (Roderick Red Elk's complete interview appears in chapter 6.)

Using a substitution method similar to what the Navajo code talkers later developed, the Comanche code word for tank was "turtle," bomber was "pregnant airplane," machine gun was "sewing machine," and Adolf Hitler became "crazy white man."

Fourteen Comanche code talkers took part in the invasion of Normandy. Two code talkers were assigned to each regiment, the rest to Fourth Infantry Division headquarters. Shortly after landing on Utah Beach on June 6, 1944, the Comanches began transmitting messages. Some were wounded but none killed, and they continued to serve in the 4th Infantry Division during further European operations.

The most well-known and most written-about group of code talkers is, of course, the Navajo, for several reasons. First, they were the largest group. Four hundred twenty Navajos were recruited and trained as code talkers, though not all of them saw combat duty. Second, their code was kept secret for the longest time, becoming declassified in 1968, so the news made more of a public splash when it was finally revealed. And lastly, and most unfortunately, many of the Navajo code talkers claimed to be the *only* "true" code talkers, entirely dismissing other natives who'd used their tribal languages to send secret wartime messages. (See the bibliography for multiple sources on the Navajo code talkers.)

It has always been the position of National American Indian Veterans that any American Indian soldier who used a tribal language to communicate secret messages to one of his fellow tribesmen during combat should be considered a code talker. Congress validated this view when it issued the Code Talker Recognition Act in 2008, recognizing that some twenty American Indian languages had been used in this manner.

Even though the Comanches and the Navajos were the only *officially* trained code talkers who devised codes within their languages for use in WWII, as many as one hundred other American Indian soldiers from as many as nineteen other tribes used their native languages to send coded communications. Many of these uses were not well documented because they spontaneously appeared on the battlefield in a time of great need where two or more Indians spoke the same language.

Among the Choctaws who brought their native tongues to war was Second Lieutenant Schlicht (pronounced "Slish") Billy of Pittsburgh County, Oklahoma. Because of high scores on intelligence tests he took after entering the army, Billy was sent to several special schools to receive training that prepared him for a battlefield leadership position. When explaining how he came to use his language with other Choctaws during battle, Billy said, "We were more of an experiment because we had it (the language) at hand right there."

Because enemy shelling often destroyed land lines, they had to use other means of communications.

"When a shell hits," Billy remarked, "it tears up your communication lines—so we had these little 536 radios. I went to school for that, so I had knowledge on how to use that. And we knew that the Germans were good at breaking codes and tying into our lines, things like that. So that was the fastest and easiest, and we had the language."

Billy said he regularly conversed in Choctaw when using field radios to coordinate military maneuvers. Quite often, Billy's Choctaw friend and machine gunner Davis Pickens was on the other radio. Pickens was usually positioned where he could do the most damage to the enemy. Speaking the Choctaw language, the men were able to communicate exact details and locations of targets without fear of the Germans intercepting the conversations.

Billy, who was also a trained platoon leader, commanded the First Platoon in Company F, known as Fox Company, 180th Infantry Division. Billy's regiment experienced more than five hundred days of actual combat in Italy and France, and several wartime articles reported on the achievements of this brave platoon. (His complete interview appears in chapter 6.)

Documentation is still being researched to determine the names of other WWII code talkers from other tribes. At the time of publication, native soldiers from nineteen tribes (not including Navajos, because they were previously honored by Congress) had been identified to receive the Code Talker Congressional medal.

# CHAPTER FIVE

# Finally Comes the Recognition

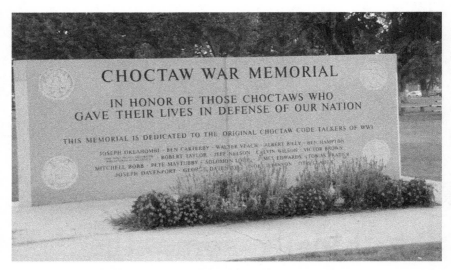

*The Choctaw Nation's War Memorial dedicated to the
Choctaw code talkers of World War I.*

Spirit of the Code Talker,
*created by artist Dan Pogue,
was unveiled in 2003
and stands in front of
the Comanche tribal
headquarters.*

What the code talkers did during World War I, and how they did it, was not reported to the public for many years, and there seems to have been no real public recognition for their efforts in the years following the Great War. Boasting or even talking about wartime deeds was not in the nature of most of the returning American Indian soldiers.

The Comanche code talkers of WWII, who served as part of the US Army Signal Corps, and other tribal code talkers were given individual permission to speak of their wartime activities, though most did not talk about it outside their own tribal community. Their accomplishments were not reported to the public.

However, the Navajos, who were part of the Marine Corps during WWII, were first recognized for their contributions to the war effort in at war's end in a publication called the *Marine Corps Gazette*. This article was soon reprinted in a publication, issued by the Office of Indian Affairs (within the Department of the Interior), that was titled *Indians in the War*. The Office of Indian Affairs had been regularly printing and distributing a publication called *Indians at Work,* which was created to publicize American Indian accomplishments and contributions to American society. During the war, several issues of this publication included native wartime facts. Fifteen thousand copies of *Indians in the War* were printed in 1946 in order to emphasize the "Indian contribution to the victory" in the Second World War.

While Navajos were allowed to divulge information about their activities, it wasn't until 1968 that the Navajo code itself was declassified by the Marines. It was then that their fame really began to grow.

Gradually, as word spread more widely about all of the tribal language codes and code talkers, the recognition came. The Choctaw Nation of Oklahoma first honored the Choctaw code talkers of WWI in a special ceremony held at tribal headquarters in 1986. The French were next. In 1989, the French government gave the Comanche code talkers of WWII an honor called the Knight of the National Order of Merit in a special ceremony held in Oklahoma City.

In 1992, the governor of Oklahoma issued a proclamation naming September 26 of that year as "American Indian Code Talker Day" in the state. This proclamation was shared with the public at an event held that day near Norman, Oklahoma, to honor code talkers. (This is covered in more detail in chapter 6.)

In 1999, Charles Chibitty, then the last surviving Comanche code talker, was given the Knowlton Award by the Pentagon, a special honor from the Military Intelligence Association. He also received other honors from state and national organizations.

It wasn't until the year 2000 that the United States Congress passed legislation to honor any of the code talkers, and the Navajos were nationally recognized at that time. That law provided for the creation of special gold and silver Congressional medals. The gold medals were issued to the original twenty-nine Navajos who developed the code, and the silver medals were issued to those who served later in the program. On the back of the medal is printed a statement in the Navajo language. It means, "With the Navajo language they defeated the enemy."

The awards were given to the Navajo code talkers by President George Bush at a special ceremony held at the White House in 2001. At that time, the president said, "Gentlemen, your service inspires the respect and admiration of all Americans, and our gratitude is expressed for all time, in the medals it is now my honor to present."

The Comanche Nation commissioned sculptor Dan Pogue to create a statue to commemorate the Comanche code talkers. His sculpture, *Spirit of the Code Talker,* was unveiled at the Comanche Nation headquarters during the tribal fair in 2003.

Even with this acknowledgement of a few of the WWII code talkers, other code talkers from the other tribes, and those from WWI, were still unknown and unheard of outside their own tribes.

## *The Code Talker Recognition Act of 2008*

The comprehensive Code Talker Recognition Act of 2008 finally addressed the issue of the *unknown* code talkers and specifically expressed the nation's gratitude for "the dedication and valor of Native American (American Indian) code talkers." The movement to nationally acknowledge the contributions of the code talkers may have begun as early as 1998 when a petition on the issue began to be circulated.

The code talker bill, H.R. 4544, was passed by the House of Representatives on September 25, 2008, and then passed by the Senate five days later. It was signed into law by President Bush on October 15, 2008, and became Public Law 110-420. The bill, as it was first introduced earlier that year, is reprinted below.

*One Hundred Tenth Congress*
*of the*
*United States of America*
*AT THE SECOND SESSION*

Begun and held at the City of Washington on Thursday,
the third day of January, two thousand and eight.

An Act
To require the issuance of medals to recognize the dedication and
valor of Native American code talkers.

*Be it enacted by the Senate and House of Representatives of the United*
*States of America in Congress assembled,*

## SECTION 1. SHORT TITLE.

This Act may be cited as the 'Code Talkers Recognition Act of 2008'.

## SEC. 2. PURPOSE.

The purpose of this Act is to require the issuance of medals to express
the sense of the Congress that--

> (1) the service of Native American code talkers to the United States
> deserves immediate recognition for dedication and valor; and

> (2) honoring Native American code talkers is long overdue.

## SEC. 3. FINDINGS.

The Congress finds the following:

> (1) When the United States entered World War I, Native
> Americans were not accorded the status of citizens of the
> United States.

(2) Without regard to that lack of citizenship, members of Indian tribes and nations enlisted in the Armed Forces to fight on behalf of the United States.

(3) The first reported use of Native American code talkers was on October 17, 1918.

(4) Because the language used by the Choctaw code talkers in the transmission of information was not based on a European language or on a mathematical progression, the Germans were unable to understand any of the transmissions.

(5) This use of Native American code talkers was the first time in modern warfare that such a transmission of messages in a native language was used for the purpose of confusing an enemy.

(6) On December 7, 1941, Japan attacked Pearl Harbor, Hawaii, and the Congress declared war the following day.

(7) The Federal Government called on the Comanche Nation to support the military effort during World War II by recruiting and enlisting Comanche men to serve in the Army to develop a secret code based on the Comanche language.

(8) The United States Army recruited approximately 50 Native Americans for special native language communication assignments.

(9) The United States Marine Corps recruited several hundred Navajos for duty in the Pacific region.

(10) During World War II, the United States employed Native American code talkers who developed secret means of communication based on native languages and were critical to winning the war.

(11) To the frustration of the enemies of the United States, the code developed by the Native American code talkers proved to be unbreakable and was used extensively throughout the European theater.

(12) In 2001, the Congress and President Bush honored Navajo code talkers with congressional gold medals for the contributions of the code talkers to the United States Armed Forces as radio operators during World War II.

(13) The heroic and dramatic contributions of Native American code talkers were instrumental in driving back Axis forces across the Pacific during World War II.

(14) The Congress should provide to all Native American code talkers the recognition the code talkers deserve for the contributions of the code talkers to United States victories in World War I and World War II.

## SEC. 4. DEFINITIONS.

In this Act, the following definitions shall apply:

(1) CODE TALKER - The term 'code talker' means a Native American who--

(A) served in the Armed Forces during a foreign conflict in which the United States was involved; and

(B) transmitted (encoded and translated) secret coded messages for tactical military operations during World War I and World War II using their native tribal language (non-spontaneous communications)

(2) SECRETARY- The term 'Secretary' means the Secretary of the Treasury.

## SEC. 5. CONGRESSIONAL GOLD MEDALS.

(a) Award Authorization - The Speaker of the House of Representatives and the President pro tempore of the Senate shall make appropriate arrangements for the award, on behalf of the Congress, of gold medals of appropriate design in recognition of the service of Native American code talkers during World War I and World War II.

(b) Identification of Recipients - The Secretary, in consultation with the Secretary of Defense and the tribes, shall--

> (1) determine the identity, to the maximum extent practicable, of each Native American tribe that had a member of that tribe serve as a Native American code talker, with the exception of the Navajo Nation;

> (2) include the name of each Native American tribe identified under subparagraph (A) on a list; and

> (3) provide the list, and any updates to the list, to the Smithsonian Institution for maintenance under section 5(c) (2).

(c) Design and Striking of Medals-

> (1) IN GENERAL - The Secretary shall strike the gold medals awarded under subsection (a) with appropriate emblems, devices, and inscriptions, as determined by the Secretary.

> (2) DESIGNS OF MEDALS EMBLEMATIC OF TRIBAL AFFILIATION AND PARTICIPATION - The design of a gold medal under paragraph (1) shall be emblematic of the participation of the code talkers of each recognized tribe.

> (3) TREATMENT - Each medal struck pursuant to this subsection shall be considered to be a national medal for purposes of chapter 51 of title 31, United States Code.

(d) Action by Smithsonian Institution - The Smithsonian Institution--

(1) shall accept and maintain such gold medals, and such silver duplicates of those medals, as recognized tribes elect to send to the Smithsonian Institution;

(2) shall maintain the list developed under section 6(1) of the names of Native American code talkers of each recognized tribe; and

(3) is encouraged to create a standing exhibit for Native American code talkers or Native American veterans.

SEC. 6. NATIVE AMERICAN CODE TALKERS.

The Secretary, in consultation with the Secretary of Defense and the tribes, shall--

(1) with respect to tribes recognized as of the date of the enactment of this Act --

(A) determine the identity, to the maximum extent practicable, of each Native American code talker of each recognized tribe with the exception of the Navajo Nation;

(B) include the name of each Native American code talker identified under subparagraph (A) on a list, to be organized by recognized tribe; and

(C) provide the list, and any updates to the list, to the Smithsonian Institution for maintenance under section 5(d)(2);

(2) in the future, determine whether any Indian tribe that is not a recognized as of the date of the enactment of this Act, should be eligible to receive a gold medal under this Act; and

(3) with consultation from the tribes listed in following subsection, examine the following specific tribes to determine the existence of code talkers:

(A) Assiniboine.
(B) Chippewa and Oneida.
(C) Choctaw.
(D) Comanche.
(E) Cree.
(F) Crow.
(G) Hopi.
(H) Kiowa.
(I) Menominee.
(J) Mississauga.
(K) Muscogee.
(L) Sac and Fox.
(M) Sioux.

## SEC. 7. DUPLICATE MEDALS.

(a) Silver Duplicate Medals -

(1) IN GENERAL - The Secretary shall strike duplicates in silver of the gold medals struck under section 5(b), to be awarded in accordance with paragraph (2).

(2) ELIGIBILITY FOR AWARD -

(A) IN GENERAL - A Native American shall be eligible to be awarded a silver duplicate medal struck under paragraph (1) in recognition of the service of Native American code talkers of the recognized tribe of the Native American, if the Native American served in the Armed Forces as a code talker in any foreign conflict in which the United States was involved during the 20th century.

(B) DEATH OF CODE TALKER - In the event of the death of a Native American code talker who had not been awarded a silver duplicate medal under this subsection, the Secretary may award a silver duplicate medal to the next of kin or other personal representative of the Native American code talker.

(C) DETERMINATION - Eligibility for an award under this subsection shall be determined by the Secretary in accordance with section 6.

(b) Bronze Duplicate Medals - The Secretary may strike and sell duplicates in bronze of the gold medal struck pursuant to section 4 under such regulations as the Secretary may prescribe, at a price sufficient to cover the cost thereof, including labor, materials, dies, use of machinery, and overhead expenses, and the cost of the gold and silver medals.

## SEC. 8. AUTHORITY TO USE FUND AMOUNTS; PROCEEDS OF SALE.

(a) Authority to Use Fund Amounts - There are authorized to be charged against the United States Mint Public Enterprise Fund such amounts as may be necessary to pay for the cost of the medals struck pursuant to this Act.

(b) Proceeds of Sale - Amounts received from the sale of duplicate bronze medals authorized under section 7(b) shall be deposited into the United States Mint Public Enterprise Fund.

Speaker of the House of Representatives.

Vice President of the United States and

President of the Senate.

*(END OF LEGISLATION)*

## *Code Talker Tribes*

Soldiers in World War I and World War II from the following tribes are known to have used their languages as codes and are being included in the Congressional Medals bestowed as part of the Code Talker Recognition Act. This information, provided by the Department of Defense, indicates the number of individuals who were known to be code talkers from each tribe.

1. Assiniboine – WWII: 3*
2. Cherokee – WWI: 1; WWII: unknown number
3. Choctaw – WWI: 19: WWII: 4
4. Comanche – WWI: 1; WWII: 17
5. Creek – WWII: 2
6. Crow – WWII: 2
7. Hopi – WWII: 11
8. Kiowa – WWII: 3
9. Oneida – WWII: 2
10. Pawnee – WWII: 9
11. Ponca – WWII: 1
12. Seminole – WWII: 1
13. Sioux – WWI: 3; WWII: 16
14. Tlingit – WWII: 3
15. Cheyenne – WWII: unknown number
16. Menominee – WWII: unknown number
17. Meskwaki – WWII: unknown number
18. Chippewa – WWII: unknown number
19. Osage – WWII: unknown number

*To successfully be able to send and receive coded messages, there has to be an even number of people who know that code: one to code the message and speak it into the radio or telephone, and a second one to hear the message, decode it, and then pass it along to the intended recipient. This author can't explain how the Department of Defense determined the number of code talkers for each language or how there could be an uneven number of code talkers for some of these languages.

## *The Congressional Medals*

Whenever Congress commissions the minting of medals, that process is executed by the United States Mint. The Mint has a well-established process for designing these medals, which was adapted for the design of the code talker medals. The process is as follows:

Stage 1   The US Mint will initiate the formal design process by contacting appropriate officials of each tribe and requesting the appointment of an individual to serve as the official liaison to the US Mint for the Code Talkers Recognition program.

Stage 2   The US Mint, in consultation with the liaisons for the tribes, will develop unique themes for the obverse (heads side) designs for each eligible tribe. With respect to the reverse (tails side) designs, the US Mint will develop a common design theme that will be adopted for the reverse of all medals produced under this program.

Stage 3   Based on the themes, the US Mint artists will produce unique candidate obverse designs and a common reverse design, focusing on the aesthetic beauty, historic accuracy, appropriateness, and coinability.

Stage 4   The US Mint and the liaisons for each tribe will collaborate on the candidate obverse designs. Each liaison will appoint a historian, other responsible officials, or experts to participate in this collaboration to ensure historic accuracy and proper presentation of the candidate designs. The US Mint will refine the candidate designs, as necessary, before presenting them to the Citizens Coinage Advisory Committee (CCAC) and the US Commission of Fine Arts (CFA).

Stage 5   The CCAC and the CFA will review the candidate designs as required by law and make recommendations, and the US Mint, in consultation with the tribal liaisons, may make changes to address such recommendations.

Stage 6  From among the final candidate obverse designs, the liaisons for the tribes will recommend their preferred obverse candidate designs. The US Mint will request documentation from each tribe supporting the recommendations.

Stage 7  The US Mint will present the recommended designs to the Secretary of the Treasury for approval.

From 2008 to 2013, the Department of Defense conducted a thorough search of its records to uncover as many American Indian code talkers as possible. During this same period of time, designers at the U.S. Mint worked with tribes to design the medals mandated by the Code Talker Recognition Act of 2008.

Finally, in November of 2013, Congressional medals were presented to thirty-three tribes, recognizing code talkers from both World War I and World War II. Unfortunately, most of the individual code talkers had already passed away by then. So, in many cases, the medals were presented to tribal representatives.

A proud nation finally said a long-overdue "Thank You" to these deserving men.

*Pictured are the front and back sides of the Congressional gold medal presented to the Choctaw Nation in honor of their code talkers from WWI and WWII. All of the code talker medals can be viewed and replicas purchased from the U.S. Mint's catalog on the Internet at: www.usmint.gov. (Image courtesy of U.S. Mint.)*

# CHAPTER SIX

# The WWII Code Talker Interviews (1992)

*Powwow grand entry in Norman Oklahoma, September, 1992,*
*where Choctaw, Comanche, and Navajo code talkers were honored.*

*Proclamation issued by the governor of Oklahoma naming*
*September 26, 1992, as American Indian Code Talker Day.*

In the early 1990s, the author was engaged in research that was meant to lead to the production of a documentary television series about the history of American Indians in the US military. As part of that research, he traveled to six states to visit a dozen reservations and a few urban communities to interview American Indian veterans.

As a part of that project, the author sent a film crew to capture footage of a unique event. In September of 1992, six code talkers from three tribes (Comanche, Choctaw, and Navajo) gathered south of Oklahoma City to be honored by fellow American Indians at the first Pow-Wow and Arts Festival hosted by the American Indian Cultural Society of Oklahoma. Dancers, singers, drummers, and artists from many tribal communities in the state attended the three-day event held at the Cleveland County Fairgrounds in Norman, Oklahoma.

A young Cheyenne veteran named Nathan Hart was the chairman of the hosting organization, and he also served as the executive director of the Oklahoma Indian Affairs Commission at the time. Hart explained the goals of the organization and what the weekend event was all about:

> The American Indian Cultural Society was formed to provide educational and culturally-related events for the general public. One of our goals is to pay tribute to Indian people who've made great contributions to our people during their lives. We wanted to honor Navajo, Comanche and Choctaw code talkers at our first annual powwow because of the significant roles they played during World War I and World War II.
>
> This is one of the few times that code talkers from these three tribes have ever been able to be together. We have heard very positive comments from each of the three groups simply because each has been able to meet for the first time other code talkers they've heard so much about.
>
> I think paying tribute to these people is long overdue. They played a significant role in shaping American history, and the United States government has been slow in recognizing their contributions.

But Indian people were quick to recognize their contributions.

Finally I'd like to say that establishing a national monument to pay tribute to American Indian veterans is very appropriate. There are so many Indians who've served in the World Wars, Vietnam, and recently in Desert Storm, and I personally feel this would be a tremendous way to acknowledge the accomplishments of these people.

Another significant participant in the activities was Comanche artist and flute player Doc Tate Nevaquaya, a personal friend of the Comanche code talkers and cultural director of the host organization who lived in Apache, Oklahoma. Mr. Nevaquaya composed a flute song in honor of the Comanche code talkers, and he performed during the event. He explained the genesis of the song.

That song is based on a Comanche riding song that I adapted to our modern melodies. The original song came from the 1800s and was sung by many of our warriors when they were returning from a hunt or war journey. They were more or less describing the success of the journey, and this particular song belonged to Chief Wild Horse of the Comanche. The old songs came from the heart and spoke to the spirit.

I played this particular song for the code talkers because it was sung by our warriors in the 1800s who had to ride long distances and faced overwhelming odds against the white man's weapons in those days, so they expressed their gallantry as warriors when singing that song, and I wanted this song to express the warrior-ship of the code talkers. When they were in battle, they had a lot of endurance, and they could go for days if they had to, so that is why this flute song is for them.

Doc Tate Nevaquaya passed away in 1996 at the age of sixty-four.

As mentioned earlier, research for the television documentary took the author to several reservations to conduct interviews. This research included one additional code talker interview that took place at the Navajo Nation Inn in Window Rock, Arizona, in the same year. He is the last code talker in the list. It was actually during this interview, conducted in the summer of 1992, that the author found out about the coming code talker honor event that was to be held in Oklahoma in September. The seven code talker interviewees of 1992 were these:

1. Schlicht Billy (Choctaw) – 1921–1994
2. Roderick Red Elk (Comanche) – 1922–1997
3. Forrest Kassanavoid (Comanche) – 1921–1996
4. Charles Chibitty (Comanche) – 1921–2005
5. Albert Smith (Navajo) – born 1925
6. William Dean Wilson (Navajo)
7. Harold Foster (Navajo)

# Interview with Schlicht Billy (Choctaw)

SB:    My name is Schlicht Billy. I live south of McAllister, Blanco, Oklahoma, and I am a full-blood Choctaw. I am seventy-one years old, and I was born in Pittsburgh County. And I lived all my life in that area even at the present time.

Q*:    (*Q = Question) Can you give me a few details about the events that lead up to you joining the military?

SB:    I knew as I read current events and newspaper accounts that we were preparing for a conflict but didn't know where, and I was at the right age. And more or less, curiosity led me to go in the service, because I knew it would be time very shortly that I would enter the service.

Q:    Before you shipped out, did your tribe or your family hold any kind of a celebration for you?

SB:    You know, we were many miles away from my people because we shipped out from Hampton Roads, port of embarkation, that none of my families were there when we shipped out. Went to Africa back in 1943, June 22, when we sailed out to go to Africa.

Q:      So there really wasn't an opportunity for your family to honor you in any way or to, you know, have a ceremony for you before you left?

SB:     No, they didn't. The fact of the distance away from where they were living.

Q:      So whenever you enlisted, what branch of the service did you enter?

SB:     When I enlisted, I enlisted in the (US Army) infantry unit, 180th Infantry of the Forty-Fifth Division. That was in 1940, September 16 of 1940. And I was shipped to Fort Sill for basic training.

Choctaw Platoon - 180th Infantry

Q:      And in speaking earlier with you, you talked about how you became a squadron leader, so you were not only just in the infantry but you managed to work your way up and you said that you always had a job to do. Can you explain just a little bit about that, how you became a squadron leader?

SB:     At the time when we were in the service, we took a test as to everything, just in general, the knowledge that you had—IQ tests. And that's one of the reasons that I guess they sent me to school a whole lot because my IQ was high enough. Although from what I see now, I guessed at a lot of the things was on the test. But, you know, I made a high score on that. From there on they always sent me to school on different phases of combat infantryman, on basic training of all the weapons in the infantry unit, and more specialized things like gas schools and how to direct artillery fire on the enemy, and a lot of map reading classes, aero photos. And I had amphibious training, ship-to-shore landings, along with a unit called Frogman's school over at Massachusetts where the Kennedys live - those people that were in high government positions in that area were trained at. And every day that we were in the service stateside, we always had some kind of school that we attended. So I had a well-rounded education in many things that some of the men didn't receive, like mountain training, that took place over in Virginia. And there was a winter training in Pine Camp, New York. That's cold country. And swamp training around Manny, Louisiana—how to survive. We worked in that area too. And as I see it, a lot of it we didn't get to use—but as it was what we did have knowledge of came in handy when the time was ripe for that type of use. And we were able to survive because I think we made an effort to really absorb what was taught to us, and we accomplished nearly all the missions that was given to us. I'll say that. As Indians, I know we had many different tribes that were represented in my division, the Forty-Fifth Division, and the units that did take part in all those phases of combat, we always accomplished our missions. And I don't see where we were running or retreating or, you know, everything we done in order. We knew where we was going—the fundamentals that we learned, the basic fundamentals came into play where we went ahead and utilized what we had to fight with, whether it be tank support or aerial bombardments or many of the other things that we learned - like scouting and patrolling, how to go about in appreciation of the territory that you were fighting on. We even had schooling on topography of the countryside. We learned many military terms on those mountain ranges like *hogs back* or *escarpments* or *base camels back*—all types of names that they had. We knew what they were talking about when the time came to use those terms. And just like in our daily lives when you know what is expected of you and you had that training, you do a better job. I believe that's one reason why we weren't afraid as a combat unit. We have 511 days of actual combat time in that book that I have of the unit that I fought with. Five hundred eleven. So with a good leadership, determination, and that discipline—even today without discipline, we're just a mob. But in that day and time, they drilled into us the things that were essential, things that we could use. And like I mentioned earlier, that it is not so much as being afraid. We all have some kind of fears, but you know, if in leadership you want to know many men you are going to come back out with in a skirmish or going on a mission. To me that was better than anything that I could think of—is that it is somebody's son that I am leading.

Q: We had talked about that earlier about the sense of responsibility that you felt to bring back everyone of those men. And also we talked about the natural-born traits of an Indian that may have been traits that were more predominant in Indians that were the qualities that you are talking about that helped, helped the soldiers, the Indians, the discipline. And, also, I would like for you—if this is true—you came from a boarding school background. How did that experience of a regimented lifestyle at boarding school, how did that assist you or enhance your abilities as a soldier? Could you talk about that for a moment?

SB: Most of us came from a rural area that one time or another, as Indians, we like to hunt and we could track things. Even a man, if the soil is wet, we could tell or have an idea how big of a man was going through that area, which way he was going. And you know how to hunt squirrels. If you are by yourself, you can do a whole lot of things. If the squirrel gets behind a tree and you're going to it, take a piece of stick and throw it on the back side of it and he will always turn toward you—basic things like that. And if we're going through an area where water is polluted and you, and you know you're going to be thirsty when your canteen runs dry. All right, we take a pebble, a smooth pebble, and put it in your mouth and you can go hours and hours and hours without drinking any water. Just small things like that help a combat man.

Q:    I think you call those things common sense.

SB:    Yes.

Q:    Can you share some of your wartime experiences, maybe something that you remember vividly.

SB:    Many of the experiences that I have—is like it happened yesterday, many of them. For instance, on invasions when you are going into a hostile shore, they had drilled us so that we knew exactly what area of the ship we was going to use to get off into the assault boats to go to the shore where people were shooting at you. Also I remember the preparation that they made. Some of the seas were real rough at times, other times smooth. But of all the invasions I had taken part in, the easiest was an invasion of southern France. Africa wasn't so bad going in there. But the war had just about ceased in that area where we was at. And the island of Sicily—that's an island between Africa and the boot of Italy—they call it Sicily. There was thirty-eight days to accomplish a mission there. We took care of those people there. British Eighth Army went up the boot going toward Naples, Italy. We made what they call an *end-run* like a football player making an end-run. We landed at Salerno, another invasion where people are shooting at you. That's below Naples, Italy. After fighting there around almost a year in the mountains of Italy- you take one mountain, there's one a little higher. They're looking down at you. A general that was in command of that fortification

for the German forces—his name was General Kiserling—
he was a man that we had to deal with. And they had
bunkers, fortifications, emplacements, everything well
prepared years and years ahead and they were there to stay.
We had to dig them out of there, maybe a platoon, maybe a
squadron, maybe a company, bombed and shelled. I guess
that is one area where we had more units fighting as allies
that I ever took part in. I had these Moroccans out of
Africa. I had these Nisei from the west coast of here in
America. (Author's note: Nisei was a Japanese term that
meant a Japanese person born in the United States and
holding US citizenship.) I remember when Pearl Harbor
(was attacked) when they put their parents in stockades
or detention camps and those youngsters or young men
that were old enough to be in the service, why they drafted
them and made a unit—they called them "Niseis," little
bitty fellows, Japs. But, you know, they made good soldiers.
We had Polish soldiers. We had the British soldiers,
Canadian soldiers, and some of the Italians fought with
us to, but not many. But as a unit, that's what we had to
fight the Germans. Remember Mussolini, he was a leader
over there—they hung him. His own people did. And the
Germans took over. That's where the big trouble was below
Naples there. We fought them people from in that area
all the way into, past Rome, Rome, Italy. I know I had to
go across that Tiber River. It's on the outskirts of Rome. I
saw that Vatican City. I saw that Coliseum, but you know
they respected the wishes of that Italian government, the
Pope, rather. Also the Americans, they respected the holy
place. So they didn't bomb and shell that out. Leading
to the city they did—bridges and roads—and after we
helped take Rome and went on past Rome. They pulled
my unit out and they sent me back to Anzio (Italy). We
got replenished with supplies, ammunition, guns, and
clothing—everything that we needed, replacements, men
that we lost along the way. And from there we went on to
southern France. We went to Naples, Italy, got onboard.

We sailed between two islands, Sardinia and Corsica. Went on between the two islands, went on to southern France where all the rich and famous goes, I guess, now. It was in that area—Leone and Monte Carlo. But, you know, that was the easiest. Nobody gave us any bad time at all. We walked in there and it was like we was the kings in there. We went right on into France. We went up the Rhone Valley toward Nancy, France. And from there everything got harder. The Germans really put up resistance all the way into their homeland. We were getting closer and closer. Allied forces were coming in from around Normandy at that time. So we had many, many good men that fought that war, especially against the Germans, and boy they were well disciplined. But they were just like anybody else, they couldn't stop a bullet. And they would go down too. There were paratroopers. There were mountain troopers. There were SS men. To me they were just humans ...

Q:     And how many years were you in the service?

SB:    Six. You see I volunteered for three. And when my time was up I was in Africa. And they told me, they just laughed, you know. As a matter of fact, I never was drafted, see. I volunteered. The draft papers—my mother sent me my draft papers in Africa. And I told my commanding officer, I said, "Hey, I have to go to the draft board." And he laughed and he says, "Six months plus—the duration plus six" So that was my status of being in the service there.

Q:     And now we are going into how you were selected to be a code talker.

SB:    I was selected? Well, the language that I have, I already knew that, the (Choctaw) language. We were more of an experiment with it, because we had it at hand right there. There was something that needed to be told to our units—either we had these powered telephone lines on the ground, but we couldn't depend on that because there was shelling all the time. When a shell hits, it tears up your communication lines. So we had these little 536 radios. I went to school for that, too. So I had knowledge on how to use that. And on flat country you could go maybe a mile or two with it. But in mountainous country, why, you couldn't get too much good communication out of it. But it served the purpose. And we knew that the Germans were good at breaking codes and tying into your lines and things like that. So that was the fastest and easiest, and we had the language. And it just so happened I could speak both languages, you know. And we had our own figures too, you know. On your grid coordinates, on your maps, battle condition maps, why we could use our own figures and relay the messages—like you want to send artillery shells to an objective, it could be a mortar pool or whatever it was. You didn't even have to say the guns. Just say, "Fire control center," and them boys would be ready to go—these combat units that are manning those guns back there. We had weapons that shoot up to twenty-one miles, those big 155 Howitzers. That's what we had. That's about the longest distance. And we had mortars that were sixty-millimeter mortars, and we had eighty-one millimeter mortars. The maximum was 1,760 yard on the little sixty mortars and we just utilized what was at hand because we had it. And one of the boys, he is deceased now, but he was a machine gunner. He had a chart of a section. That's the boy that I used to speak (Choctaw) with most of the time when we wanted communications to the next unit. He'd relay it for me. I would tell him what I wanted since I was a platoon leader most of the time. I had forty-seven men under me that I was responsible for. And when I would call in to him the location where I was at and where he was at and I would have him get the best fields of fire because he can do the most damage to the enemy. And he had full authority to take that position wherever it was at. And one thing I had too in my favor, as a unit leader, they usually let me have anything I wanted—tank fire, or close support, airplane bombing or even ships at sea—they even sent me to school to learn how to control that fire from the ships, those sixteen-inch battle wagons. They called it JAN Grid System, JAN: Joint Army-Navy. That's what I trained for that too. So I had a pretty good knowledge of the things I had to do.

Q:     Tell us a little about how you used the Choctaw language to explain or to use the code for military terms whenever there wasn't a word in Choctaw that described the military term. How would you improvise? Be sure and when you are telling me this, say, "As a code talker I used the Choctaw."

SB:    I would say artillery; you're talking about large caliber weapons. When speaking about artillery you want a certain amount of concentration. It is said (in Choctaw) "Tenapo hochito." That would be the large whatever you have at your batteries. It might be 105 millimeters. It might be 90s. It could be 155, or it could be chemical, chemical mortars was 4.2 millimeters. We could call in our own figures, what we wanted, what would be best. If it's a wooded area, maybe wanted a tree burst—we let them have a tree burst. And boy they sure do a lot of damage, with tree bursts. Because not much you can do when they burst in the air and scatter.

Q:     Can you in your Choctaw language give just an example. Again, I know you just did, but another example of maybe an order or something that you would use in code and then translate it into English.

SB:    Okay. For instance, you were sent on a combat mission. In other words, you want to bring in a prisoner, and about the only way you know how is to cripple him and carry him in, or else you want to try to kill him and try to get the information from this enemy. And you can relay it this way (in Choctaw): "Hatak ish benah. Stish na tagee Oh chayahou. Bring him back alive. Don't kill him." And that's what we would relay to the other men, whoever was with us, you know. You might have three people with you or maybe a dozen people. But they want to know. You have a set pattern where all needs to know that's going on. That is where we would try to do in all of our attacks. You know where the line of communications is, where your water supply would be, where your ammunition dump is, and where your food supply, K rations or C rations or whatever it is, first aid stations. We knew that. So, it took all hands ...

Q:    As a code talker, was there any, is there anything that stands out in your memory as being frightening or funny or a memorable experience that you had as a code talker?

SB:   Yes, I know on one occasion, as a code talker, we were up in the mountains of Italy, around Venafro (Italy). This particular person that I was talking to, we were in what we called "pup tents." You have one half of the tent and that is a shelter half and you have the other half. You put them together and hopefully keep you dry. But it rained so hard and the tent was so soaked that he was sitting up, and he says, "You know why they call this a pup tent?" And I said, "No, why?" He looked at me and he said, "Dogs have more sense than to sleep in one of these." (He chuckles.) Just, things like that. And on another occasion where we were fighting these other Germans way up on top of a mountain. We got halfway up the mountain and this young Indian, he says, "I'm going up and loosen them up." I said, "What do you mean, *loosen them up?*" He said, "I am going to get the cobwebs out of his head," he said. He was standing, looking up there, not concerned, and I said, "Hey, get down, boy. They're going to kill you." He said, "Well, we own half of it, don't we? I am going to go over to get the other half of that mountain." Things like that, to me now, when I think back, he had some kind of humor about him that he survived, in that particular battle anyway.

Q:    What honors or awards or medals have you received and what did you do to get those awards?

SB:    The awards that I received - mostly everybody that has been in combat and has injuries caused by the enemy that sheds blood. Why, you start out with the Purple Heart. I am sure that everybody has seen a Purple Heart. Then you add the Bronze Star. The Bronze Star is … Many of the assignments that you receive toward advancing your unit or accomplishing the mission, if you do it satisfactorily, in a way that you been taught to do, and it is something out of the ordinary that you did, maybe using the knowledge of the area that you are fighting on or maybe outwit the enemy, you receive a Bronze Star for that. It is a medal similar to the Silver Star.

Q:    You said you had your own coordinates. You are talking about … You had a Choctaw relationship or a Choctaw word for those coordinates. Is that what you meant?

SB    The figures.

Q:    In other words, you related those figures in Choctaw.

SB:    Yeah.

Q:    Okay, good.

SB:    I didn't bring all of my awards, like the Victory Medal. Everybody that's been in that war brought the Victory Medal and stuff but these are the ones. (He holds up his Purple Heart.)

Q:    Okay, look at the monitor. Are we ready?

SB:    This is the first medal that I received for being shot through the foot. We were advancing on the retreating enemy, and I was shot through the foot and we had this sulfa medicine. All we do is kind of clean it up a little bit and put that sulfa and tape it up and go. I mean it throbbed a little bit, but we kept a-going. And that's your Purple Heart. Along with this you get a bar that goes with it. Here's a bar that goes with it. (He holds that up.) That's the purple one here. I've got three oak leaf clusters in lieu of four of these (Purple Hearts). See I have been injured … First time they give a medal. The next, don't care how serious it is, all you get is this little oak leaf cluster to go with it on the bar, so there it is right there. (He holds up the medal and the bar so the cameraman can take close-up shots of them. Then he holds up another medal.)

Q:      Okay, tell me about this.

SB:     This is a Silver Star medal and this is a third highest that the American government gives to the soldiers that fought against the enemy, and it is known as, on the back side here is an inscription. It says, "For gallantry in action." And this was given for the leadership, and this is the first one that I received. All the days that I had command of the different units, different groups of people that come and go. Many times that they sent me a leader, he didn't last too long. He would either get killed or else he was wounded or they would replace him. I was usually the one that had to do the replacing. And that was the first. And it has a bar also that goes with it. (He holds up the bar.) There it is, this bar here goes with it, and they have got a lapel, a small replica that goes on your lapel of your uniform. And this oak leaf cluster in lieu of another Silver Star like this, they give me one of these that go with this bar. That was when I happened to be fortunate enough to take the German fortification away from that … And this is what that is for, that little bitty black-looking oak leaf cluster. Instead of giving me another medal, they give me this one. (He holds up these medals so the cameraman can get close-ups.)

Q:      When you were wounded? Can you relate that story? Was that the pillbox … The German pillbox?

SB:     In action against the Germans, on their own homeland, that was March 17, 1945, and it was in the Siegfried lines. There was a main fortification, and that was their homeland. They were defending their homeland from those bunkers. Some of the doors, as we captured this particular one that they, the doors were six feet thick, steel reinforced concrete. And firing machine guns and different infantry weapons at it, just knocked the paint off. That's about all it done. That's how thick it was. And I had the mission with the unit that I commanded to take that German pillbox. And it was interlaced with twenty-six other pillboxes. I have a book here that shows an overlay of the map where these fortifications were placed. They were placed in such a manner that it took care of each other. One of them shooting straight ahead, flanking fire and it looked impossible to go through any part of that—machine guns. You see, they had a cyclic way to fire the twelve hundred rounds a minute, their machine guns. We used them slow firing—five hundred rounds a minute—that's what we were firing at them. They had twelve hundred rounds in those German Schmeissers (a type of submachine gun).

And we were fortunate enough to go in and accomplish a mission that we were assigned to, and there is an open country, something similar to that, everywhere I go-even today, I was looking around about this countryside, I can see how in the world would I attacked this position? Hillside or smooth grounds or whatever. It just is something that I learned that I always refer to it, some of the things that I have seen- how to attack it if I had to, you know. And that's one of the things we learned in a line of appreciation. And there was a little draw, just kind of a fold in the ground, that I saw. We went down in what we call *Indian style*. We didn't go all in big bunches spread out there in the open. We would go one at a time in there like a snake going through. That's after I got my men organized. We got started all right, and then we were pinned down. They (the Germans) really raked us good with artillery, mortars, and machine guns. Of course every one of them was helping one another. Just like a sewing machine or something— those burp guns. Anyway, when we got to this position where we were pinned down, that's when we took to the little old fold in the ground, crawling on our bellies, to get to this first fortification. I went to that door, and they had a big old lock on the door. I dropped to the ground and I said, "I'm not going to do any good here." So I thought and looked, and it had a little old ventilation system, something similar to that on top of this bunker. It was just like a cellar, where great big, bigger than this room here, where they had twenty-six bunks, and then they had generators and dynamos, food, and all kind of supplies in there, running water, and they were there to stay. And when I saw what was happening there, I went around to the back door, thinking it might be open. Still locked tight. So I looked around and I saw that ventilation. And I come back down, and I saw this little opening where this machine gun barrel was sticking out. They had a periscope sight in there, like a submarine, you know. The periscope sight would be sticking up, and they could look into the scope. They didn't have to expose themselves and I knew I was in trouble if I didn't do something with it. So I went on around and I threw a smoke grenade or a fragmentation grenade in there first. Nothing happened, nobody came out or nothing. So I had a smoke grenade that I tied on my belt and I pulled it out and I threw it in there. That's when I heard them about get choked down in there. That's when they began to come out of there. They was hollering, "Comrade." And I had that 536 radio on and I radioed back to my company. I said, "I've got a tiger by the tail here and I can't turn him loose." (On the other end of the phone line) He said, "Don't turn him loose."

When we got squared away and reorganized, more and some of my men came right on where I was at. We occupied the outside positions but I secured it the best we knew how, right around that area. We had good cover. And when the smoke cleared, I sent those German prisoners back. I said, "You guys get on out of here. Get on back where I come from." (He points behind himself.) I figured some of the men would shoot them down, but they didn't. So

I radioed back to the company commander and I said, "I have prisoners going you way. I have sent them back there." He said, "All right. We'll take care of them." So, we were busy, twenty-six of them (pillboxes) ahead of us, all around about us, that needed to be taken care of, cleared out. So we went ahead and accomplished our mission and about that time, the German force had begun to pull out of their positions and went out in the open, and they re-shelled the position they just lost. That's how they do counterattack. They catch you in the wide-open space. Boy, they let you have it with artillery. And that's what happened. That's the last round-up for me that day. That's why I was wounded. What I was doing, the German emplacements, some of it was about eight or ten feet deep that the German engineers had dug for them for the route of escape. And they had some ladders sticking up from the hole to the top and I was checking one of them out, and I heard that big 170 millimeter mortar coming in, and boy it hit. And I had blood shot all over me. I looked like I had measles. Next round came on in and hit the top of that. That's when they took me out of there. That's when my war days were over. So I received two medals that day, the Silver Star of oak leaf clusters plus another oak leaf cluster for the Purple Heart. On the invasions where you are invading enemy territory, they give you a little bitty arrowhead. When you make an invasion, see that little bitty black arrowhead. (He holds up another medal.) That's what you receive if you're surviving. But anyhow I got the invasion of Sicily, Salerno, Anzio, and southern France where the people are shooting at you when you're going in there to them. That's what that's for. (He holds up the medal and turns it so the cameraman can get a close shot.)

Q:      After you were wounded, how long did it take you to recover?

SB:     Two years, fourteen days, on the last wound - partially paralyzed the left side of my body.

Q:      And back to that battle, how many Germans were lost that day? Did you have a count or anything?

SB:     That's one thing that is hard to determine after a battle. There's so many people involved in destroying the enemy that those that are in direct contact to that area where they have been shelled or when you are attacking, that would be the easiest way of accounting the casualties of the enemy, would be counting after a battle. That's the best way, but so many things involved in there. If there's a concentration of artillery on a given target, it is going to involve civilians and everybody else that is in the way there. But the Allied forces always did warn these large cities to move out of there. And they gave them warning to move out of there. They are going to bomb it.

Q:      Mr. Billy, when you were involved in that battle, were you afraid or were you just cool under fire? What was going through your mind?

SB:     I was concerned about the mission, the route of our approaches, and my line of communications that we had it pretty well intact because of that 536 radio we had. But the concern, as many battles as I had been in, is bringing and leading the units out without too much casualties. I believe that is the best answer I can give you, is bringing all you can out from that particular battle, because if you don't find an enemy, you are going to go find him. It's like a bully in town, if you go looking for it, you're going to find it.

Q:      What are the other medals you have with you?

SB:     Let's finish up on this one. This is a Presidential Unit Citation. That's awarded to a unit that accomplishes a mission, helping other units that may be in trouble. In this particular case, we were in Alsace-Lorraine. That's the northern part of France. That's around that old Maginot Line, First World War positions. And the Germans had surrounded the French Seventh Army, and we were called on to help relieve the pressure and get those men out of there, the French troops. And each one that took part in accomplishing that mission, we were given his Presidential Unit Citation. It has a blue field, gold borders, and it goes on your uniform. And this (he holds up another pin that displays an Indian in headdress with two crossed arrows) goes on your lapel of your uniform, dress uniform. It is in the Choctaw language. "Tanup Nonakeah Asteah." Ready in peace or war. That is what this is. That goes on our uniforms.

Q:    That's good.

SB:    I have some ribbons. We didn't' receive any medals for the other than just the ribbons that goes on your uniform. Victory Medal bar and that Asiatic duties, European goes on this, right here it is, the little bitty bar that goes on this uniform to … (He holds up another ribbon.)

Q:    What was that again?

SB:    It is that European theater of operations. What it amounts to.

Q:    Now I'm going to ask you, did you experience any prejudice against Indians? Was there any kind of stereotyping?

SB:    I think we were all happy that we could rely on each other. That's what combat is all about.

Q:    Let me restate that. Did you experience any prejudice in the military?

SB:    None whatsoever. I didn't experience prejudice toward my leadership. We worked in harmony. Everything I asked of those young men, they just automatic went right ahead and did the best they could. That's all you can ask of any combat man. I had a good team.

Q:      You said that you had three or four members of your family in the military. Talk about that.

SB:     All that I can relate to my immediate family would be ... I had three brothers that served in the service, but one of them served in the Ninetieth Division that came in on Normandy invasion, and the one that was with me, he got killed in 1943, July 18, when he died. He lasted eight days in combat. But then, I had a younger brother, he came back. He was an Eighty-Second Airborne paratrooper. Other than that, why, I didn't have any immediate family other than cousins, but they were different branches of service, like the Marines, and we weren't together in combat. They were scattered all over the country, all over the world.

Q:      When you returned, were you given any type of ceremony?

SB:     After I returned back to the United States, I couldn't ask for no better treatment. Everybody just couldn't do enough for us. Those that I came in contact with, like most of the folk, paralyzed or we were battered. If we want letters written, or somebody was there to help us, or read to us, you know. Anything that they could do for you to make you comfortable. And they had a lot of help too at that time, they had the WAVES. They had the WACs. They had volunteers. They had their regular nurses. They had the doctors. They had the war boards. I mean I couldn't ask for more. They even shined my toenails even. I mean that's the kind of treatment we had.

Q:      You might explain ... hospitalized for the two years ...

SB:     Yes. When I came back to the United States, the first place they sent me to was Fort Devins, Maryland, the hospital there in Boston. I trained there too about a year before going overseas. And I knew the country pretty well, and they were nice to me there at Fort Devins. Then, to Walter Reed, that is in Washington, for further treatment of all paralyzed veterans. And after we got better, they sent us to

Camp Edwards for a short stay there, and on to O'Reilly General Hospital, Springfield, Missouri. And they had all types of entertainment there for us too when we got there. They had these big name bands back in the '40s. Les Brown and Cab Calloway and different people like that, entertainers. And they just more or less let us take it easy and we would take treatments and those of us who could walk a little bit, somebody would be helping us to gain our strength back. Everywhere we went people would try to feed us something: train stations, bus stations. They had facilities all ready. I don't know who sponsored all that. I can't remember that far, but they really took care of us.

Q:      Can you tell me the extent of your injuries, maybe show where you still have shrapnel?

SB:     Yes. To start out with, on my left arm here I have a piece of steel there that has been there since 1945, and they told me it would never hurt me, but it does hurt me. It stings and, when wintertime comes, it aches. But I can live with that. It's in there. And I have got one in my shoulder, way down deep. And it seemed that I had cancer at one time. Told my wife about it. I knew better than that. There's a piece of steel in there, and it's got a growth around it, and the doctors told me that it would be all right. It wasn't necessary that they take it out. They could go in there deep and get it. And I had shrapnel in my head right there (points), but there they took skin grafts off of my leg and fill this up and I had an X there where another piece of steel. I'll tell you a story about the hospitalization over in Italy. They had a hospital, Thirty-Sixth General Hospital they called it, was at King Umberto's Palace, and they converted it into a hospital. And that's where they sent me. They had gold fixtures in their bathrooms and things like that at the time I was there. And when they stay there long, when they took the shrapnel out, and when they gave me a skin graft, kind of fill those up and, put skin grafts on my arm too, see. (He points to his arm.) Where the steel went in and I took the graft out of my stomach right there and …

Q:    Was it mostly for shrapnel wounds they gave you treatments?

SB:    Yes, yes. Bullet wounds. I heal pretty fast. Got shot through the foot there one time too, right there. But it healed up. I used to heal rapidly.

Q:    When you came back stateside, did you have any problems readjusting to civilian life? Was alcohol ever a part of that?

SB:    No, I am fortunate. I didn't have any problems, even when I entered the hospitals, different hospitals. That's one of the questions they usually asked me. Do you sleep well? Do you have nightmares? Different things that bother you in combat days. I told 'em, "No." That's one thing that I haven't experienced is having a hard time adjusting to civilian life. I have always been busy anyway. I believe that's one of the keys to life is staying busy. You can always find something. Helping others, somebody else, you know. Read a whole lot.

Q:    So you think you had a good readjustment because you kept yourself mentally and physically active?

SB:    Yes, that's right.

Q:    Do you see an interest or a need for a national Indian veterans memorial?

SB:    I've always thought about that some years ago for I believe we ought to have a community where … maybe centrally located or where the need is. We know the need is everywhere. In my particular tribe we don't have as many Choctaws in there compared to the western tribes, you know. But you know it would be well if we had good counselors stressing education because without education we're going to have a hard road to travel. Our youngsters,

I'm talking about. Old timers like me, why, it's not so bad. We adjusted years ago, how to take care of our own selves. But these young ones, drug abusers, alcohol, lack of education, that's one thing I would like to see our leaders in high government positions to ... In the leadership from a local level to help all young people because we aren't going to be here but a very short time ourselves. Somebody is going to have to do something, and that something is education.

Q:     Going back, can you restate for me in your words, I believe we need a national Indian veterans memorial?

SB:    I do believe that we need a veterans memorial for the future cause of our young people in education and everything related to it.

Q:     How many other Choctaw code talkers did you serve with?

SB:    In the beginning, scattered throughout the regiment, a regiment of men is composed of around six thousand men—in that we were sparsely scattered according to your ability to take care of the job that you were assigned, maybe communications, and we weren't all in a group, but those that were able to converse with one another (in Choctaw), well that's what we did, because we knew the language and there was no problem there. Like we knew our figures. We could read and we could write it. And relate what was in store for us.

Q:     But you don't know the exact number that served with you, Choctaw code talkers from Oklahoma?

SB:    Well, to start out with we had around seventeen Choctaws, but like I say some of them were transferred to headquarters, some of them were sent off to school, like radio school, liaison people, and some of them were sent to ... as runners between companies sending messages, you know. This individual would send message to the next unit or something, and that's how we survive, is just using our language because we had it at hand. We didn't need to go to no classrooms and study. We just talked to one another just like we did back home.

Q:     That you were the ones defined as Choctaw code talker.

SB:     Yes, as far as we know, I haven't heard of anyone else that was in the area where I was at that carried on a conversation. Like artillery training there was a Captain Crane that taught me to be a forward observer and to have communication with the fire control center in directing artillery fire on enemy targets. But the man died up in the mountains of Italy. He got hit with shrapnel, but we may start something in Pittsburgh, a little community down there that have asked me to help the children in a spelling bee, about two more months away, I suppose. I had some of them enrolled in my class and we took first prize among all the Choctaw communities round there, like Antlers, Clayton, even the city of McAllister. They have got Choctaws in there at a little school that I taught over there to read the Choctaw language and how to use it. Well, we came out first place and we had fifty-four sessions of spelling bee contests. And we came out first place. We work harder we may take it all again this year.

Q:     So you carried on your tradition of using the language as a teaching tool. Thank you for sharing with us.

SB:     Well, it has been my pleasure. I enjoyed it. I have enjoyed everything I have seen today here.

Q:     That's good.

SB:     The hospitality is good around here.

Q:     Can you tell us about this photo? (He is shown a WWII era photograph.)

SB:     That picture of the platoon that I was in was taken at Fort Sill, and it was September 16, 1940, when that was taken.

I was a squad leader. Starting out I had twelve men in the unit that I had. That's the first assignment I had as a squad leader. I was in basic training at Fort Sill, just a beginner at that time. And from there we advanced to Camp Barkley, Texas. That's in Abilene, Texas. From there we went to Louisiana. From there to Fort Devins, Massachusetts, Camp Edwards, Maryland. Then to Pine Camp, New York. Then back to Fort Devins. Then back to Camp Edwards. Then the port of embarkation. That was in Hampton Roads, Virginia. I remember the ship that we sailed on had ten thousand troops on one ship. And the name of the ship was Freddie Funston. It took us twenty-two days to go to Africa. We landed at Oran, Casablanca. Then we were in training in Africa, the northern port of Africa. They had the French units there that we trained with, getting ready for the invasion of the island of Sicily. In the meantime nearly all of those men right there were transferred out to other places where they were needed for further training. (He holds up a photograph of his Choctaw unit.)

Q:     (As the camera begins to pan across the photo ) If you remember, can you call some of their names out?

SB:    That's what's hard about it right there. The first one we see on the far left ...

Andrew Perry. He's deceased, killed in the service. Um, I don't remember his name now. Anyway, this lower picture we just passed over is Laurel Conn. That one, his last name is Baker. Forreston Baker, this big fellow with a weapon. That's Einer, E-i-n-e-r, Martin, that man right there. I don't remember this other fellow's name either. I can't even recall these names. They didn't stay with us very long.

Q:     Who was this?

SB:    Yeah, he was our Jeep driver. He ran over a mine and got killed. Louis Wade, I remember him. He was a mailman. Delivered mail to the frontlines and his name was Louis

Wade. He ran over a mine and he was killed. (He holds up a newspaper story with the headline: "The Platoon That Suckered Siegfried Line.")

Q:      What was this?

SB:     The platoon that suckered the Siegfried line, that's a unit that I commanded that took the first pillbox away from the German forces that one day's battle there. (He holds up another photo of two soldiers next to a mortar launcher with their backs to the camera.)

SB:     That particular day I am on the right making preparation for the route of approach to the German position.

Q:      What are those concrete pylons? Are those bunkers there?

SB:     That's *dragon teeth* - that hampers the tanks. It makes them raise up and it's, the underside of your tanks is softer, the steel is softer and more apt to blow up.

# Interview with Roderick Red Elk (Comanche)

Q:      Please tell me your name, your tribe and where you live.

RRE:    My name is Roderick Red Elk. I live in Lawton, Oklahoma. My tribe is Comanche.

Q:      How old are you and when and where were you born?

RRE:    I am seventy years old. I was born out in the country in Cotton County. That is south of Walters, Oklahoma. Born in 1922, January.

Q:      How did you become a code talker?

RRE:    There was a man that came down and talked to several of us for the purpose of joining the army to be code talkers. And we all went in around—this was December, '40, when he was recruiting us and we got sworn in. I got sworn in January 1, 1941. And we went from there to Fort Benning, Georgia, and took our training—just regular basic training with the army. And after basic training, then they started us on the different types of communications: how to operate, tear down, and repair the telephone, radio. And then we had to—a lot of military terms there is not Comanche word for them. So we had to sit down and figure to a name for each, for instance, like gun. We just have one name for gun and that is *stawoy* (approximate spelling). It just means a gun. When you get in the military, you have all types of guns—you got your artillery, you got your small arms, you got your machine guns, the different caliber machine guns—and we had to work out a word for each one of those different types of weapons. The same way with airplanes. We had to identify airplanes. We had a word for airplanes. But we didn't have no word for bomber or fighter or a transport and we had to get together and come up with a name that everybody could understand and would relate to what we were talking about. Just for instance, like a bomber. We have words for airplane but a bomber, there's no such word for a bomber. So we got together and kicked it around. And we come up with the word in Comanche, *esnoab*, which means pregnant. You know, those bombers carried those big bombs under them like they had big bellies like a pregnant woman. And that's what we called a bomber.

Q:      Can you give me another example? Say a sentence in Comanche and give me interpretation in English.

RRE:    I have got one better than that I believe. Let me see. Let me straighten it out. Machine gun would be a better one. Okay. Just for instance, I'm with a regiment and we are getting a lot of machine gun fire, so I have to call back and relate the message to the artillery and point it, pinpoint it on the map for them. I tell them—I'd be speaking Comanche. I say—(Comanche words). I am saying this machine gun is really giving us heck, really shooting us. So then I tell them—the artillery will have a man over there that speaks the same (Comanche) language. I tell him. Then he relates it to the guns and say, about five or ten minutes, and then all the machine guns are silent—the machine guns that's firing on us.

Q:      What is the Comanche word for machine gun?

RRE:    (He speaks in Comanche.) In Comanche, that is a "sewing machine," the only way we could associate that with a machine was *a-rat-a-tat-tat,* and you know, how you're sewing how that sounds. That sound is what we associate the machine gun with.

Q:      What honors or medals have you won?

RRE:    Well, I just received one yesterday at the Comanche Nation. They gave us an honor, a little plaque. And I received one from the French government. I think that was in '89. And before that I received another plaque from Comanche Homecoming. That's a group around Walters—at the annual powwow—and they give us a plaque. That's the only awards, just recently. Are you speaking of awards while we was in the army?

Q:      Yeah, your service medals.

RRE:    Oh, gosh. I can't remember them all. We were in five major campaigns so that would be five stars. Each campaign is a star, and I had a good conduct medal. You know you have to be a soldier and your conduct has to be good so long before you receive one of those. And every campaign that you are in you receive a medal and a ribbon for that. The Bronze Star is another one, and every time you get a Bronze Star, then they put you a cluster on it the next time. And if you get over five, that's about all they can get on there, they have to give you another award. And naturally, the Purple Heart, and that's when you are wounded. That's about all I can think of right now.

Q:          Do you see that there is a need or an interest in a national Indian veterans monument or memorial to be erected in honor of Indians who've served in the military, and if so, where do you think it should be located?

RRE:        Yeah, I believe we should have a monument erected, but as far as the location goes, we would have some controversy there, because, you see, you got all different tribes in different states. I think each one should—each state should erect one in their state where they're—it's like the Navajo code talkers, now they are all a big bunch. I think they should have one there. And all the code talkers in Oklahoma should have one in Oklahoma, in a centrally located place.

Q:          How many Comanche code talkers did you start out with in your group and how many are remaining today? That's the last question.

RRE:        We started out with seventeen, and in the time we entered the war, there was only thirteen of us left. And up to date there was only three that actually went to war, and there is one, another one, there's four that's left, that's still surviving that was in the code talkers.

Q:          That's what we needed.

Cam:        Can we get from him one memorable story?

Q:          Okay. Is there a memorable story as a code talker, either frightening or funny? A lot of them shared funny little anecdotes about the code talkers' experience.

RRE:        Yeah, I got one good one. As you know after we hit the beach we just—wherever the infantry hit resistance we would stop and we would clear the resistance, and then we would go. And we did that the first day from six o'clock in the morning until dark. So we pulled into this little—there in France they got what they call hedgerows. They use that for fence to keep your cattle and stock in. So we pulled into this place, and just as we pulled in, I said, "We are going to spend the night. You all settle down for the night." And about that time we hear an artillery go off and you know, after you been there awhile you can tell whether they are close or far, and this one was getting closer. And man, I scrambled for the nearest hedgerow and luckily there was already a foxhole dug there. So I just dive in this foxhole. I say, "This would be a good place to spend the night." So I just take my helmet off, and I laid my gun across my belly and laid flat on my back and went to sleep. I wake up the next morning in good daylight, I look on the other side on the foxhole, and there sits a German soldier with his rifle lying across his lap—his eyes wide open. And I just froze. I didn't know what to do. I thought well, one of us has got to make a move. So, I grabbed my gun and swung it over to him and he never moved. So I go over there and check him and sure enough—I slept with a dead enemy all night long and didn't know it.

Q:      How did that make you feel?

RRE:    I just showed the dead German how fast I could get out of the hole. (He chuckles.)

Q:      That's good. Well, we are going to let you go because we know you have got what, twenty minutes to get back.

RRE:    Yeah, it don't take long to get there.

# Interview with Forrest Kassanavoid (Comanche)

Q:      Let's start with your name and your tribe.

FK:     My name is Forrest Kassanavoid. In Comanche, that is
        pronounced _Kass-a-na-vo-da_ (approximate spelling).
        _Kasa_ means "feather" and _navoda_ means "to mark," so
        my grandfather's name was Kassanavoda, which meant
        "marked feather." And I am a Comanche Indian of the
        Q'ata band and my sub-clan is Tipicui. Tipicui is Comanche
        that means "mountain of rocks."

Q:      And where do you live?

FK:     I live at Indiahoma, Oklahoma. That is in western
        Comanche County, twenty miles west of Lawton.

Q:      How old are you and where were you born.

FK:     I am seventy-one years old. I was born at Indiahoma. I was born in a tent. My grandmother was the one that brought me into the world.

Q:    What are some of the most memorable experiences you had as a code talker? Is there one or two that stand out?

FK:    I think the one that stands out the most with me was a message that was sent by one of the code talkers. It was not me but one of the other fellows. It was a message that was sent by Brigadier General Theodore Roosevelt Jr. who was the assistant division commander of the Fourth Infantry Division, and he sent a message back to the command ship when they made their landing at Utah Beach in Normandy, when he realized that they had landed in the wrong spot. The Eighth Infantry, which was the first wave, made a landing and through some error from one other service, either the coast guard or the navy who was bringing the troops in, they made an error, so they landed at the wrong spot and the reason they sent the message is that they didn't want the Germans or the enemy to know that they had made a wrong landing.

Q:    What about an experience where you were involved?

FK:    Where I was involved? Well, this is kind of a humorous— but I think one of the experiences that I remember that sticks in my mind the most is a friend of mine who was a code talker. One night we had moved up from our command post and we dug in along a hedgerow. Well, this one fellow—his name was Perry Knowubad from Cyril—he was one of the code talkers. He says, "Oh, I'm getting too sleepy. I am not going to dig a foxhole tonight." So he didn't dig one. So that night we got a raid by the Luftwaffe, and they were dropping butterfly bombers on us, so everybody was jumping in their foxhole, except him. He didn't have one to jump in. So he jumped into the garbage pit that the unit before us had dug, and they didn't cover it up. And boy, there was all these tin cans in there. And when he jumped in there he cut his body up, cut his feet and everything. And after he came out of there, they saw he was bleeding, so they sent him to the aid station, and he went there. And after they treated him, they tried to pin a Purple Heart on him. Of course, he had had several before, but he says, "I don't need that. I didn't get wounded. I got cut up by jumping in that garbage pit where all those tin cans were." (He laughs.) And I think that sticks with me more than anything. He was my buddy, and a close friend of mine, but it was just the humor of the thing that stuck with me so long.

Q:      That's good. And then one last question.

FK:     Sure.

Q:      What medals or honors awards have you won for your service?

FK:     Well, I think the one that—there's two of them that I think the most of and one is the European—the African-European-Middle East campaign ribbon with five campaign stars on it for the campaigns that we served in Europe. Now I think that is the greatest. That means more to me. And I think the second most important one that I cherish is the Order of Military Merit, which was awarded to us by the French government in 1980, I think it was 1989, here at the state capitol in Oklahoma City.

Q:      One last question. Tell me your feelings as you come here for these two days to be honored with the other code talkers.

FK:     Well, the thing that I was—I think it is great that they are doing this today in this time, but until just recently they began to recognize the accomplishments of these code talkers. And I felt that this should have been done some years ago for the simple reason that many of our Comanche code talkers have already passed on. There was seventeen of us, and there is only five of us living today who actually, you know, were code talkers. Now, there's two that didn't go overseas with us. One fellow lives in California. The other one lives in Oklahoma City. But no fault of their own, they were discharged, you know, for medical reasons. Us three that went over—there's only three of us left, and I felt that there's already been twelve that has passed on, and I felt that some recognition should have been given while those men were still living.

Q:   Okay. That's what we needed. We really appreciate it.

# Interview with Charles Chibitty (Comanche)

(At the beginning of the interview, Mr. Chibitty holds a framed certificate he had recently received.)

Q:        Mr. Chibitty, can you tell us about that award -what it means and when did you receive it?

CC:       We got this Saturday evening, around about 4:30 at the Old Comanche Grounds where when I was a little kid about, I remember, about five years old. Its west of Lawton - a little town named Cash, and its two miles north. They call it the Old Craterville Park. I danced there in the late '20s when I was small, and Major General Hugh Forrester from Philadelphia brought it down and honored us with these certificates from the government, and give it to Forrest Kassanavoid, Roderick Red Elk, and Albert Nahquaddy and myself.

Q:      Okay, we'll begin the regular interview. I am going to ask
        you to tell us your name and your tribe and where you're
        from.

CC:     My name is Charles Chibitty. I am a full-blood Comanche
        Indian, and I was raised near the Wichita Mountains
        near Lawton, Oklahoma, in Comanche County. But now,
        after the WWII, my girlfriend came down to see me and
        I went to Tulsa for just a week, and I am still there after
        forty-seven years. I live in Tulsa, made my home there and
        probably be there the rest of my life.

Q:      Can you tell me, as a code talker, what are some experiences
        or an experience that stands out in your memory?

CC:     Well, there's a lot of things that I could talk about. But the
        most thing that I never did forget, that we had a boy from
        New Jersey, and his name was Mullins. I never did know
        his first name. He was one of the replacements that came
        to us. But the boys nicknamed him Moo because he liked
        to read a funny book, and he had a funny book that had a
        Moo Mullins in it. And that night, he was sitting just arms
        reach from me, and there was a lot of mortar fire coming.
        And we dug down in a hole, and when it quieted down,
        we got back, and another one hit, and I ran to the nearest
        house, because they had a basement. And I looked back,
        and he was slumped over, and I ran back and picked him
        up, put him on my shoulder and carried him to safety. But
        I didn't know it, but the medics said he had a direct hit in
        his heart with the shrapnel. That I never did forget. He was
        a good friend of mine from New Jersey, and he also showed
        me a picture of a little girl that was his daughter, and he
        never did see her. She was born after he was sent overseas.
        And I never forgot that one man.

Q:      As you have been here these several days visiting with the
        code talkers, sharing stories—can you share with us some
        of what you shared with them?

CC:     After fifty years—way back in 1941 when it started with the Comanches—you see the Navajos in the Pacific had a big territory to cover and there was over two hundred—about two hundred of them. The Comanches—you take France and Germany, you could put them in Texas and Oklahoma. That's the difference. There was twenty of us, and fifteen of us went overseas. And I never did forget the words that we used. They have a—as I understand it they could write theirs, you know. We can't. You have to talk Comanche fluently, and then the other one would listen to it, and he could write it down in English, and that way the Germans could listen all day, and it has never been written. I think here the university is trying to put it down in a book, but I don't think they have ever really been successful with it. If we had to do it again (serve as code talkers) , we probably would. Let me give you an example. It's kind of funny in a way. We got a bit of a laugh out of it. My older brother (Bobby) was in Normandy same time I was. The next time I met him, he came in from southern Germany, and his division moved next to mine. Me and him got together, and we were sitting there and he says, "Where can I get hold of one of you (code talkers)?" Because I was with the Twenty-Second Infantry Regiment with the Fourth Infantry Division. He says, "Let me have that telephone." So, I got a hold of one (Comanche) boy named Yekashak—he was with the Eighth Infantry Regiment. And my brother, told him (jokingly), "I am your enemy." (Chibitty says *enemy* in Comanche.) And then he said, "I understand your Comanche language." He said—(Chibitty says a sentence in Comanche.). "Go ahead and talk, I'll write it down." (More Comanche words.) And, Yekashak was one of us (code talkers). He (Yekashak) said, "Who are you?" And then my brother said again (Comanche words). "I am your enemy." And Bobby said, "I am (really) Charles' brother. My division moved close to yours and I am just talking to you." My brother got a big kick out of it. (Chibitty laughs.)

Q:     So there were other members of your family that served in the military?

CC:    I had a first cousin there, Larry Sawpitty. He was just raised up across the road from me up there, north of Lawton. And I was surprised to see him leave because he was always a homeboy, but he talked Comanche fluently, so he went with us. And it wasn't just before the Sentinel breakthrough if you are familiar with it, and after we took the Cherbourg Peninsula—then there was a line there and we moved up and we laid telephone lines on the tanks. They had markers on there. And that night, before the breakthrough came on, we got a lot of shelling from the Germans with 88s. That was a deadly weapon—artillery. And my little cousin, he dug a hole, and he dug it next to a tree and that 88 hit the top of that with an air burst, and it really shot him up pretty bad—one through his head and one through his leg—and he laid there, he said, for about two hours before they found him. The next morning, I got a word from my sergeant from Coleman, Texas. He said, "Your little brother got hit. If you want to go see him, go ahead, take the Jeep and go on back." And it wasn't over five miles, maybe a little over that, where the hospital was. And when I got there, they had already flew him to England. And then a few of the other boys, one in particular, Yakisha, Paul Yakisha, he would always say, "They ain't built a bullet that can shoot me." And then when we was at old Germany, he got hit in the back, just grazed him like somebody got a knife and cut it. He jumped up and run and when they had him on a stretcher, behind a Jeep, him and another white boy that was wounded, and while it was snowing and sleeting and it was bad and it slowed down, and the two medics in front was looking forward, he jumped off and came back to where we was. So they clamped his wounds up with them clamps and he just stayed around headquarters then. Boy, we got after him. You ought to have went on back where you could have a hot meal and a good bed.

Q:      Do you think that the Comanches being such fierce warriors—you come from a long line of warriors—do you think that had anything to do with you being good soldiers, well disciplined?

CC:     That's one thing that our commanding officer and this major general I was talking about—he was a second lieutenant fresh from West Point that came to work with us at Fort Benning, Georgia. Now he is a two-star general. He was with us last Saturday at Lawton. And he was with us (in 1940) working on how to say things that we couldn't say (in Comanche). And as far as warriors, they always tell me the Comanches were lord of the Plains from Mexico, Oklahoma, and Kansas, you know, and a little bit up to Colorado. And I've heard a lot of good things, a lot like the Battle of Adobe Walls. They knew they (the Comanche warriors) was going to get killed, and they said that little Gatlin gun came out (brought by US soldiers). So they sang the song and went in, and all of them got killed. We carry that song high. We don't sing it just anywhere, unless it's for warriors. And as far as it has being—I don't know, when they asked us to do what we did (to be code talkers), we gladly did and we probably would do it again if they asked us.

Q:      Do you think—just kind of building on that one statement you made—you know American Indians have always either been stereotyped or there has been a lot of prejudice in this country against them, so why do you think American Indians are always first to serve the country.

CC:     That's something that I always wondered, because in my younger days I went to the Fort Sill Indian School out of Lawton. And they had—if we talk Indian they would punish us. But we would get around and talk to each other in Indian, and when we seen them coming we'd hush up. But not only at Fort Sill. There was other schools. But later on in years now, they try to make us—I was caught in between the old traditional way and where modern ways kind of come up, and I am going to be seventy-two years old pretty soon.... Give you an example that happened to me at—(years ago) I was the only registered voter in a group of (white) glass workers. They called us glazers. There was five of us sitting there. And this man up in Tulsa—he was running for (political) office—he went ahead and shook hands with those white boys, but he didn't shake hands with me. But he didn't know but I was the only registered voter sitting there. And somebody said, "You going to vote for him?" I said, "So and so, I wouldn't vote for him if he was running for a dog catcher." Those things show up. But now I think everything is going to settle down, and everybody is going to try to love each other.

Q:      So, even in light of that prejudice, as far as you're concerned, would you still serve your country, you would still go?

CC:     I would, yes.

Q:      What makes the difference—I mean why would you feel that way?

CC:     This is our place. I made a speech for thirty students from Sicily, and I sang them a song, a Native American song. I still attend those religious—that was here before white man ever come here. We talk to that man (pointing up). We call him (Comanche word) "our Father." We didn't know (Christianity)—and then when they (our people) heard the word—I used the word "Jesus" in that song. And one of the students questioned—he said, "Where did you learn that word, *Jesus*, at?" And naturally, it kind of hit me a little funny. I said, "Well, a long time ago." I said, "There was an Italian man. He got in boats and he was coming this way (to America). I think he was lost because he hit over here somewhere. They call him Columbus. And he had a book. They called it a Bible. And different churches went different ways, and different Indians joined different churches—Catholic, Protestants, and others—and we learned it from that book. Now we use what we learned of what happened (in the Bible) years ago, and we use that word, *Jesus*, because he was kind to everybody. He listened when you asked something from his God. And we use it in our Native American Church. We've always used it."

Q:     That's good. Now will share with us your feelings about what is happening here at this honoring of all you code talkers.

CC:    It was a wonderful feeling to know that the Navajos and the few of us left here, the Comanches, that we did something for our country. Like it said in some of these deals we get, maybe we saved a lot of lives when they couldn't break the Indian language, the Navajo code talkers or the Comanches. If we made that big contribution, I am glad I was part of it.

Q:     Can you share with us some of the things you learned as a young boy—your traditional teachings?

CC:    I was taught when I was a young man—always hold your head up and, most of all, always respect the elders. Always—not only your mother or uncles or aunts—but all elders. If you see an old man, go over there and say a good word to him. Then you get that feeling that one of these days when somebody be good to me, I am going to be a man. I wanted to go where I could go and do things, and be proud of what I am going to do. Just like when they asked us to be this Comanche code talker. It made me proud that I would go, and I learned from them to always hold your head up and do what you think is best. And they said in that Native American Church, they got a line: "It's a road of life." When you stay on that road and hold yourself up, and if you kind of fall off that road a little bit, people are going to bite at you a little bit. But if you can stay on that road of life, straight life, you're going to be a man and you're going do what you want to and be good at what you do. That way, that's what I got encouragement from folks that I would go and do what I was asked to do and do it with all the best of my ability.

Q:      Before you went away (to war), did your tribe or family hold any kind of traditional ceremonies for you?

CC:     Before I went overseas, they was coming close. We knew that. And Mama and them (my family) has always been a religious group of people, the Methodists. And they had a big church service for me. And also one man that lived a mile east and back at north of Lawton -and ever since I was little, he always called me son-Old Man Abe Manachacha. He said, "Before you go, son, I want you to come up to my house to see me." I had my uniform on. I went over there. We went in the back of his house. We sat down where his old peyote ground is. He put four peyotes on the ground and he prayed. He said, "God give us this medicine to use when we need it. I am going to put it in this little pouch." He says, "I want you to tie it around your neck. It is going to take you over there, and it is going to bring you back. When you get scared, you get fear, you take one out. Chew it a little bit. Put it in your hand and pray to God Almighty. He is going to take care of you. With this medicine for Indians to use when they are in need or fear—when you fear, use it." And when my little cousin got hurt—I just got through talking about him not long ago. I felt fear because a lot of artillery and mortars were coming in. And I sat down and I talked, prayed, and my little white friend that sat by me, he sat down with me. He listened. And I told him what I was doing. So I used one of those medicines. And when we got into old Germany and stuff didn't do right, I did the same thing. And I came back (from the war). That close. Several of my brothers got wounded. But I was close. That old man's prayers went with me. When I got home, I heard he had passed away. I will never forget him.

Q:      Okay. That's good.

CC: Yesterday over there, they gave us these (points to a ribbon), and then all the veterans danced with us. There was one Comanche—a young man, tall. He said he served in Vietnam. He said, "I heard about you all my life, Charles Chibitty. That name, I heard it. I got to meet you now. I am going to give this to you. Wear it for me. I earned it. My grandfather is George Espany." I used to play ball with his grandfather. He was older than I was. I was young. I was catching. He said, "I am his grandson, and I am going to give this to you. Put it on when you put on your uniform, put everything, your other ribbons you got, your four battle stars and everything. Wear that. I earned it. I am going to give it to you." That's where I got it. You see we didn't have that extra infantry badge, but we were with the infantry all the time. And he knew that. He said, "I am going to give it to you. I am a veteran from Vietnam." So I thanked him and I said I would wear it with pride.

Q: That's beautiful. We really appreciate it.

# Interview with Albert Smith (Navajo)

Q:        Tell us your name and your tribe and where you live.

AS:       My name is Albert Smith. My tribe is Navajo. I am from
          New Mexico. I am living in Gallup. My home is in Red
          Springs.

Q:        Please tell us about your being president of the Navajo Code
          Talker Association. Tell us a little bit about the association
          and when you took over the presidency.

AS:       The association, the Navajo Code talker Association, was
          formed in 1971. At the present time we have thirty-five
          active members, twenty-two non-active members. Those
          are the ones that come to see us maybe once or twice a year,
          and then out of the four hundred code talkers, we just have
          about a hundred that we come in contact with. The others,
          we're not sure. And out of that, eleven have been killed in

action and a little over a hundred have passed away since then, since the end of the war.

Q:     And when were you elected president?

AS:    I have been president for nine years, off and on, but steadily for the past nine years.

Q:     How old are you, and when and where were you born?

AS:    I am sixty-seven years old. I was born on the reservation before there was any hospital in the Hosta Butte area, and later on I lived in Red Springs. That's where I'll be moving to when I retire from the public life.

Q:     What do you do? What has been your vocation?

AS:    I was a schoolteacher for forty years. I retired in 1989. I have gone from Zuni Reservation, taught there three years. I was in Chimawa, Oregon, for fifteen years. I spent one summer in Alaska when they were forming the Head Start. I was helping them out. And since that time I moved back to the Navajo reservation to head one of the adult education, at one of the agencies. And then I retired. Now I am doing mainly the code talker work.

Q:     What are some of the details of the events that led up to you joining the military? Did you enlist or were you drafted?

AS:    I enlisted. The thing that came about was, they were having military induction at the school where I was. I was just fifteen, but one of my uncles was in the Philippines at the time and another uncle was on the east coast waiting to go to Europe, and we were debating whether we would be next, and we wanted to stay together, so I moved my age two years up, and the same way with my other brother. That's how we got in, but it didn't last very long because of the five Sullivans that were killed in a battleship. They were all lost in one heavy bombing. And so that is what split us up. We didn't serve together.

Q:     Before you went away to the service, did your family or tribe hold a ceremony or event for you?

AS:    I went from school. I had a deferred, deferred over a month before school was out before I went in, but in the meantime my dad had some other things done for us.

Q:     What branch of service did you go in to?

AS:    I was in the Marines. This is where the code talkers were in. They were all in the Marines.

Q:     Can you share some of the most notable experiences that you had over there that stand out in your memory?

AS:    Why, it was just a special duty that we had to do. We were regular Marines, and then this was a special assignment that we did. We weren't always code talking. We did the regular duties as regular infantry Marines, like I started off as a radio infantryman with Four Company. After three battles, I moved up to the regiment, and then just before Iwo (Jima) I was assigned to the Seventh Fleet, Admiral Nimitz's command, to do my work. But I did everything from communications center, a runner, message center and guard duties and whatnot, besides my radio work.

Q:     And how were you selected to be a code talker?

AS:    All of us, those of us that were Navajos, we were assigned— after following our basic training, we were assigned to advanced training. That's when we were assigned to this special Navajo communication group, and that's where we memorized—you had to know enough English and also enough Navajo so that you wouldn't spend so much time learning the language at the same time that you were learning the new code. See, it was a code, but it was the language and then a code, so that even if you spoke Navajo, you couldn't decipher the language, the coded language.

Q:     Was there any particular instance, as a code talker, that was frightening or funny or that stands out in your mind?

AS:     Well, at first it wasn't quite noticeable but later on like on Iwo, the Japanese tried to interfere by cutting in on our radio frequency, so we had more than one radio, and this changed the frequencies that we were receiving and sending, and to confuse this, they (the Japanese) threw everything at us, tried to knock our communications center, but our communications set-up was in different, a distance apart from each other so that if one was hit you could always move into another radio set.

Q:     What awards or honors or medals have you won, and what did you do to receive them?

AS:     Well, the only award that I received was from the general during my service with the Seventh Fleet. It was a Commendation Letter from the commanding general of the Fourth Marine Division and also from the Fifth Amphibious Corps.

Q:     What was that for?

AS:     That was for being on the radio continuously for twenty-four hours, and something that never got into the record was that they had to give me a shot, one of those sample shots by the medical (corps) to keep me going, because that's how much communication was going on—and there was just two of us between the shore and also the radio ship, the command ship.

Q:     So they had to inject you with something?

AS:     They had to five me a sample of whiskey.

Q:     Ohh!

AS:    Which was illegal, but then and under this condition they had to do it to keep me going. And then they had a guard by, almost constantly by us. Like when we were in one—there were two of us, so one was inside while the other was receiving in another area and if the person was busy and another call came in, both of would be busy and so there was a guard with us at all times.

Q:    While you were in the military, did you perceive that there was any prejudice against you because you were an Indian?

AS:    There were times it showed, but it didn't bother us. We had a duty to do and there was enough of us that if I was by myself it might have made a difference, but there were more than one. There were always two or four of us in a unit together, so that if somebody was using those tactics on us we didn't, it didn't bother us.

Q:    I need you to tell me that again, including something about the prejudice in your answer.

AS:    I mentioned there was some because sometimes there was a slang remarks but we got used to it. Just like for example sometimes they would call us *chiefs* and we weren't chiefs but then it was just one of those glancing remarks. And sometimes as we pronounce a word, we'd get percussion on it, but then it didn't bother us.

Q:    Whenever your service was over was there any kind of a homecoming celebration that your people gave for you?

AS:    There was none. I just came home and spent one week at home. This was during Christmas. And I went back, if there was something, maybe if I had waited longer they might have given me something, yeah. But, I just went directly back to school and I didn't want to use my GI to finish high school so I asked if I could take an exam and try to go through, finish my high school as soon as possible without using my GI Bill, and I was allowed to do that.

Q: So how long were you in the military?

AS: I was in during the duration with two, a little over two and a half years.

Q: When you came back home did you have any kind of problem readjusting to civilian life?

AS: No, I didn't have any difficulty, because that was one of the reasons I left, because of the problems. I had the summer before I worked at eight different jobs, and there were some other social problems, but they were minor so it didn't bother me.

Q: Okay, so when you enlisted it was maybe because of social pressures. Did alcohol have anything to do with that?

AS: No, I didn't have any problem to go into that before. I wasn't involved in any drinking. I didn't like it.

Q: So then after your military experience, do you feel like maybe you matured a little bit more so you were able to adjust? Did you have as many problems when you came out as you did when you went in—pressures?

AS: No, I didn't. It was the old—I wasn't in the community. I was away from the community. I was living out on the reservation about four or five miles out. And the only time I went into town was, oh, for groceries or for food or just to shop for minor things. Otherwise I didn't have anything much to do with the town.

Q: Were you wounded in any way?

AS: No, that's one thing about that *doing* I had. I had some close calls but I went through it without a scratch.

Q: Do you see that there's an interest in building a national Indian veterans memorial? And if so, where do you think it should be located?

AS: Yes, I see that. There is an interest.

Q:     In this last question, I am going to ask you to say something in your tribal language and then translate it back into English.

AS:    We had, for example—we didn't have a term for *hand grenade* so we developed that and called it potato. And in one of the other major items was, see the code was based on the basic military terms, the essential terms, and we used the—when we were talking about the planes, in our code we'd be talking about the birds. And if we were talking about the ships, we'd be talking about the fishes.

Q:     Say that in Navajo.

AS:    (He speaks a sentence in Navajo.) Amphibious tractor—(continues in Navajo)—carrier—(continues in Navajo)—submarine.

Q:     So, submarine for instance—what did that really mean in Navajo?

AS:    It means an "iron fish."

Q:     Use a whole sentence using submarine as if it were in a message you would give in Navajo, and then translate it in English.

AS:    (He speaks a Navajo sentence.)

Q:     Tell me what you just said.

AS:    I said we were using the term the *iron fish* when we were using torpedoes to—for a landing or for a destroyer services to bombard the coastline.

Q:     I think that's all we need. Can you think of anything?

AS:    Oh, yes. And I don't know if this would help. One prisoner of war—the Japanese found out that they had a Navajo who was a prisoner of war and he was a Navajo, they found that out. And they did everything to him to try to have him decode our messages, and the only thing that he got out of it was that the men were having eggs, and the only thing that he could arrive at was the pilots were having breakfast. (He laughs.)

Q:     Good. Can you tell us about your ribbons and medals?

AS:     (He points to the ribbons on his shirt.) This is my Commendation for Iwo Jima. This one is a Navy Unit Citation from the Navy department. This one is a good conduct medal. This one is a Presidential Unit Citation, one for Saipan and one for Iwo, with the stars. This one was defense. These are my battle stars for campaign ribbons. This is my service in Japan, and this is my overseas, overseas duty and my Victory Medal, and this one is for another overseas duty, only in a peacetime. And this patch I have here (pointing to his right sleeve) is our logo (Navajo Code Talker Association). It indicates the short rainbow with the eagle feathers at the end. This is signifying a good travel, a safe travel. This is a shield, which they used before in combat, and it was also used—what I am doing right now, communicating. And it was also used in the legend when the two twins (Navajo legend)—I don't know if you have read about it—the two twins were communicating trying to locate their father, and there was a spark that came to them just like the dove in your traditional (Christian) ways, and this is the staff showing the various stages of our tribal development. The bottom stages, these are usually the base, the bottom, is black signifying the dark ages. Then the next would be a blue bar, indicating the time when the waters came, like even in your biblical stories. Then the next bar is a yellow indicating that his was the time the development of electrical lights. And then the last bar, the last one would be white and that is where we are now, using cosmic rays.

Q:     That's really interesting.

AS:     (He indicates the yellow shirt all the Navajo code talkers wear.) The yellow color signifies a pollen, which Navajos use in their prayers. And our cap used to be blue signifying the sky, but it faded so we switched to the Marine Corps league, which is red, with the writing on the side.

Q:     Can you take it off so we can see it up close?

AS:    (He points to pins on his cap.) Now, on this side, these are my honorable discharge buttons from the Marine Corps. And this is a Congressional pin by Congressman Richardson, and this is the unit that I served with, the same as this one on the side. So this side the tribal seal and my forty-year pin from the government service and the youth from the Native Association. I help out and not only me, but most of the code takers, we contribute to the advancement of youth by being a promoter for scholars, promoter for good health—we have talks, we present talks, and we also help the youth to help them to attend, like this one youth that is going to be with the American Indian Science Society in Washington, DC, in November. So we are going to be sending one individual there, and I received it. This is thirty-year, and this is a pin from the Apaches, from the White Mountain Apaches.

Q:     Very good. Thank you.

# Interview with William Dean Wilson (Navajo)

Q:        So the first thing I want to know is your name, your tribe, where you're from …

DW:       My name is William Dean Wilson. They just call me Dean for short, and I come from Navajo country—Navajo land. They call me Dineh as that was what our people were called way back, according to my dad. But this, I don't know how far back now, he used to tell us there is no more of those people. They are all gone. So somewhere they were called Navajos (enemies), so there is a different story about that name. Some Spanish people say, "Oh, we call them that because they used to steal our horses, women, and stuff like that. (He laughs.) Which is—I don't know how true that is—but it is a name that stuck with the people. But there are a good many of them now that they call themselves Dineh, like up in Alaska, and they talk like we do. So some of their singers come down for our powwow, and their songs have Navajo words in them. So that's neat.

Q:     Tell us why you are here.

DW:    Why we are here in this barn, big barn. We came to Norman by invitation, to meet some code talkers from this area - Oklahoma. So, here during this powwow, we are honoring these folks who did the same kind of work that we did, only over in Europe during the WWI and WWII. So that's a celebration that they're having here honoring those people. So we came to do our share, meet with them and talk with them and see what the situation is that they were in during that time.

Q:     Can you tell me how you were chosen as a code talker—how they actually chose the Navajo code talkers?

DW:    After the first combat engagement, we understand, on Guadalcanal—that's down there in the Solomon Islands—the enemy were catching, deciphering, many of their important messages that they were sending, so that they (the enemy) knew what the next move was going to be of these Marines. So word came back—what shall we do? Well, at the same time, this Philip Johnston, he claimed he was a son of a missionary, had some idea about using the Navajos to be brought—I understand a couple or maybe four Navajo boys—down to Camp Elliot. That is where the Marine headquarter was for the west coast. That is just about thirteen miles northeast of San Diego. And he introduced them to the brass there and gave them an assignment to transmit to one another, one over there *(pointing across the room)*, and one over here, and wrote them a message. Sure enough they got it, just like that. So that idea became a reality. So they send word back to the Marine Corps headquarters in Washington. So the commandant gave an order to go ahead and recruit, instead of regular sixty men—that's a platoon—just recruit thirty and run them through the boot training, and see what they can do on making up this code. So that's how I came on. They recruited at Fort Wingate High School, and Fort Defiance High School (both on the Navajo Reservation). These were boarding schools, Indian boarding schools. That was up north. I was up there. I always say the only reason I got in was my teacher kind of pushed me into it because I was the bad lot in the class, ninth grader. The rest were all tenth, eleventh, and twelfth graders. Anyway, I don't know how many—about fifty I guess—went through physical training or examination at Fort Defiance Beatrice Hospital. Quite a few of them couldn't make it because they either can't see too well or had something wrong—the eyes, and this and that. That's why you hear the ad, you know. What do they say in the Marines? (The few, the proud, the brave.) So only thirty came through. So we got on a bus. Incidentally, this year is our fiftieth anniversary—May, 1942—they put us on a Greyhound bus and headed out to San Diego. Thirty of us. Somewhere, maybe in Phoenix, one of the thirty jumped off. So when we got to San Diego, there were only twenty-nine of us. So we went through boot training, all that, rifle range shooting. These guys did pretty good. They got a lot of compliments on their training—rifle, pistol shooting, and all that. And after that, of course, they sent you to what they call that advanced training, which at that time was at Camp Elliot, about thirteen to fourteen miles northeast of San Diego. That was where the Marine base was. Before Camp Pendleton came about, that was a big ranch, you know, Margarito Ranch. So that became Marine Corps base later, and at this Camp Elliot, of course, we went through, they taught us all phases of communications. They taught some of us about telephone, how to lay telephone wire, climb poles, climb all that in the jungle, and radio—how to transmit by voice, how to transmit by Morse code, and then how to use all these flags, you know, like the navy use. You know, it's a long pole with a flag, one way, dit, and the other way is dash, you know. So this was another way. Then, of course, the Navy uses this on the ship, those blinkers. So they taught us all that, but during all that time we spent some hours trying to make up the code. We get together and went through the alphabet first. What shall we call letter A, letter B, and on down the line. We want to use the shortest Navajo words. So different ones made suggestions. So for A, we use the word aunt—*olachi,* and B–(Navajo word), and on down the line. Then we went into military personnel, officers, and then the various shops and equipment, all that—airplane, submarines, the whole bit, and some military terminologies. We all find some Navajo word for them, so that by the time we got down we all went through a course while we were making this. We knew what they were. So then after we finished it, of course, they ran us through what they called field exercises, right there. Some went out to ship at sea; some went into the air with the airplanes; some just right there in the area in tanks or, you know, boondocks, and sent messages one way or the other. And they must have come out pretty good, because they okayed everything. None of this ten-day leave for us, they said. Boy, they shipped us out right now. That was about October, 1942. They sent two guys from this original "twenty-nine" back to the reservation to recruit some more for the same operational signal course. Some more guys came right after us, and others, a little later. So, they all claim that they were one of the "twenty-nine" when they really weren't, you know. See our "twenty-nine," we made up the code real quick-like, and we went overseas and they spread us out into different combat units that were already out and did what we had to communicate. So then, eventually when more of these people came about, they added some more to the code. They made up some more—added words one at one time. I believe it was after Iwo Jima, they called us over to the Big Island of Hawaii, and there we went through all the new code that added to the ones we made up, so that we had to study that and then use it there before we went back to the units that these guys came from. So that was how the code was used. And, when it was unclassified in 1968 or 1969, all kinds of stories started up—that we even had bodyguards, which was a joke. We were just another jarhead out there, you know. We did mess duty. We did guard duty—just about anything that our fellow Marines did. The only thing that they used to identify us with was we were radio communicators. That's all—voice—except that we *yak* in our language, which was coded. They taught us how to decipher and cipher a message. And there were other areas that they taught us, infantry duty. So we were just kind of oriented in all phases, in case.

Q:     So you were highly trained outside.

Dean:     We were not just code talkers, you know. That was just one of the duties we had to—in the event a general or someone wants to send a special message, maybe highly classified message, to aircraft out there or somewhere or in the area where they are fighting. That was the time that these guys would get together. We only used two radios. One was where you had to crank it out with a generator. The other one was operated by a battery. That was the one we carried in front of us. And the pack in the back, it was kind of like a burro—pack burros. So that was the way the whole thing came about.

Q:     Okay. Thank you. That's all we need.

# Interview with Harold Foster (Navajo)

*(No photo available)*

Q:      Where and when were you born?

HF:     I was born in the hills of western New Mexico on the Navajo reservation on May 15, 1925. And when I was five years old, I entered a school. They put me in school in Toadlena, New Mexico. I stayed there from kindergarten to eighth grade. After I finished, I went to Fort Wingate. This was a vocational school. It was from ninth to twelfth grades. May 15, 1942—that's when I graduated from high school. In March, 1942, I enlisted into the Marines. And then it took me three months—March, April, May—to have my parents decide if they would let me go into the service. When I was still at Wingate, one Sunday afternoon, it was December 7, 1941—that's when the Japanese bombed Pearl Harbor—we were in the living room when it came over the radio that the Japanese bombed Pearl Harbor. Then the President of the United States, Franklin Delano Roosevelt, and the Congress declared war on Japan. Since then I decided to go in the Marines because of the posters they had at Fort Wingate. They had these posters that showed the uniform that was ideal for me to wear if I had to go in the service.

Q:      Recruiting posters?

HF:     Yes, posters at Wingate. Because where I lived, there's nothing. It's way out on the reservation. So it struck me as the one I wanted to wear. It took me three months for them to say (okay). The second month in April they decided, "okay let him go, let him go in the service," and my mother said "No, we need him here." And my late father said, "No, there's nothing here. He's finished school, and he can work anywhere, but there's no jobs."

Q:      So that was when you went in?

HF:     No, it was still April—see March is when I enlisted—March, April, May, that's when I went in, right after I got my graduation. Finally we got the witnesses together. I did not register for selective services. I wasn't old enough. And if you're sixteen or seventeen—I was sixteen when I volunteered. Like I said, it took me three months to have my parents to say okay. And then on the rules and regulations they said, you need three witnesses—so we got the missionary, the trader to get them together for my parents to give their thumbprints. My parents are uneducated. They never went to school—they don't know how to write. Thumb prints was the only thing they could do.

Q:      When you were asking for your parents' permission to enlist, what did they say?

HF:     They figured that since I graduated, they said, "Let him go ahead and defend the country." See I was a Catholic, so we'd have to have a priest to come and witness, and the priest was the interpreter—he explained certain things to them, to my parents, so it was important for him to come.

Q:      So, are you still Catholic? Have you ever included traditional Navajo teachings in your life?

HF:     Catholic, being Catholic is secondary, but my Navajo religion is part of who I am that I'll never forget, because they're the reason why—they have this certain protection ceremony, which they have done for me and for other Marines (before we went into the service). When I got back, they had another one to purify my soul.

Q:      So who did that for you?

HF:     This one medicine man from my area.

G:      Did your parents come to this ceremony?

HF:     Well, my parents went over there and they brought me, and He (the medicine man) did the ceremony.

Q:     What is that ceremony called?

HF:     They called it Squaw Dance (modern name). It takes several days. That's the Enemy Way ceremony—what it used to be called (traditional name).

Q:     Why is it called Squaw Dance? That's not a Navajo word.

HF:     Well, see, part of the Squaw Dance is with the men and women dancing together. There a lots of people who come (to one of these dances).

Q:     So, somewhere someone decided to call Indian women squaws.

HF:     It comes from a (white) trader or someone like that.

Q:     So when you left here, how did you get into the code talkers?

HF:     Let's go back. After I graduated, after they signed me up— my parents signed the agreement allowed to go in—I went to Albuquerque. That's where I got my first physical. And then there was about six of us that went to Santa Fe. And then at Santa Fe High School, we went to the gym for another exam. There were thousands of kids same age. Some of them were inducted to go into the Army, to go into the Navy, Air Force and the Marine Corps. They were all there getting their physicals.

Q:     Was that Santa Fe Indian School?

HF:     No, not the Indian school. Santa Fe High School. I got my physical there and then they told us they'd allow us a couple of days to go home, that's when I had my ceremony for the protection. And my parents dropped me off on Highway 666 (near the edge of the reservation). I caught the bus there, and then I went over to the train depot in

Gallup. That's where my package was, which included the ticket, the meal ticket, to go into LA.

Q:      You went to Los Angeles?

HF      Yeah, we stopped on the way- Winslow, Flagstaff, Needles, Barstow. We got there in the morning. We drove all night, I mean we rode the train all night. Have you ever been to the LA train depot?

Q:      Not to the train depot.

HF:     That train depot waiting room is big. That thing was full of kids the same age as—I just turned seventeen—same age as me. Some were older. And then we waited for an hour or so. At ten o'clock—we got in there around 7:30. We waited until ten o'clock in the morning, and they said all the kids there are going to San Diego Naval Base or the San Diego Marine Corps Base. They called our names off, and we boarded the train. We waited there until the afternoon, and then we started.

Q:      You were on the train waiting from ten o'clock to three o'clock waiting?

HF:     Yes. We finally moved, and we didn't get there until ten o'clock that night. Then they got us in these cattle cars, three-deckers. We board the cattle cars and they took us to the Marine Corps base in San Diego. It took us eight weeks for boot camp.

Q:      What time was it when you finally got to the base?

HF:     Two o'clock in the morning. It was two o'clock in the morning when they showed us how to make up our beds. This is how you make the Marine Corps bunk. We just got to sleep and got up around three thirty and started again.

Q:      Where along the process were you selected …?

HF:     I'm getting to that. The next day, we got our uniforms, and we sent our civilian clothes home. That same day, after we ship our clothes home, we got our *good* haircut. They kidded us: "How do you want your haircut, chief?" See, I was the only Indian in that platoon, the rest were all white kids.

Q:      So naturally they called you "chief."

HF:     Yeah. So a little later, they gave us a rifle, and then we started off. At four o'clock is our revelry, four thirty we're supposed to be out there for calisthenics, day in and day out for six weeks. In that six weeks we went to the classroom to learn our general orders, attend general orders, know how to swim, how to take our rifle apart, how to hold the rifles. Then we went to night class where we learned all about what we're supposed to do—how to defend ourselves. It really wasn't very different from my parents used to say when they were teaching me how to do things. You do this, and you do this, and you don't do that. What I did when I was civilian wasn't very different from this except being away from home. On the third or fourth day I, after long class work, running, everything, I was laying there resting there thinking, *Why, why did I join?* Then I thought to myself that I joined because I wanted to defend my people, my parents, my relatives, the reservation, the state, and the United States of America. So if it wasn't for my parents I wouldn't be with you. So I have to start there. I kept that in my mind. Some of these kids, white kids, couldn't take it. They were bawling like a calf calling for its mother.

Q:      Did you have a sense that was the main reason why you went in?

HF:     That's the main reason why most of these code talkers, even these veterans, these Navajo veterans, signed up for the service.

Q:      Defending the homeland. It's a different kind of patriotism.

HF:     Well, it's not different. It's all in the same line—there's no difference. If you think about it that way. It's just like going to a church—the church and the ceremony, they pray to one. So this was like that.

Q:      Did your father or grandfather or other part of the family serve in WWI or serve in the military?

HF:     Okay, let's go back. This (Navajo) Chief Manuelito is my great, great grandfather on my mother's side, great. And how he conducted himself was pretty much down to me how to conduct myself, how to take orders, how to give orders. I had an older brother, he was in Normandy, and my oldest brother was a code talker too, and my brother-in-law was in the Air Force.

Q:      So growing up, you heard stories about Manuelito?

HF:     Yes.

Q:      Okay, so back to your experiences.

HF:     Okay, like within those six weeks, we had to learn how to do judo, how to defend ourselves, and after the graduation— the last two weeks, you spend at the rifle range. I knew how to shoot, anyway, when I was on the rez (reservation). And I knew how to take care of rifles. So the only bad part of it—I'm small. Some of those guys are taller than I am—six foot two, six foot three—and I'm only five foot seven. When you go into the prone position, I almost broke my arm off, the way they wanted you to hold yourself. Because my body structure is shorter. Even in the standing position, I don't have any trouble. But sitting or kneeling, you have you have to sit down and rock back and forth. Especially when you get down on your belly, and he says, "Get down a little more, chief." So 340 is the possible score you can get on the shooting range. I missed two. I used to hunt prairie dogs, squirrels, everything that's on the reservation. That's because all those are good eating. Now all the prairie dogs have fleas with rabies.

Q:      So let's go back to the training.

HF:     When I was growing up, I was with the Boy Scouts. That's where I learned the dots and dashes. Morse code. So in the service, everybody had to take that. So knowing I was going to be a Navajo code talker, that didn't faze me at all. But they did tell me, "You're going to be in the communication." So the scores I made were pretty good. Some of those boys were going into the SeaBees, to serve on aircraft carriers or heavy cruisers, stuff like that. After we were assigned to go to extensive training, some were shipped over to Florida for their Navy SEAL school there. Some of them went to Air Force, Marine Corps, different branches. I got my order to report to Camp Elliot. It didn't state on there what kind of assignment.

Q:      Where is that?

HF:     It's about thirty miles from San Diego. And I report there, and that was dots and dashes communications school. Then later I was transferred to Camp Pendleton for more field and class work. That's where, when I report to Camp Elliot, they say, "Okay you going to be in the Navajo communication."

Q:      When was that? How long had you been in?

HF:     Let's see—May 20—that's when we were at the boot camp—after eight weeks, that's when we start to get into the classroom. The instructor, the communications officer, which was a major, said, "Okay, this first lieutenant's going to be in charge, but you'll have two other instructors." So when we got into a classroom, they give us a folder, which the first twenty-nine had set up. Let's go back on the how that code was set up. When the first twenty-nine—a man by the name of Phillip Johnston was on the reservation when his parents were missionaries. He was here when he was four years old—he played with the Indian kids, because there's no other white kids around. So he learned a little of the language. They said he was an interpreter, but when I saw him, he doesn't speak fluent Navajo. In 1919, he went to WWI, in Germany and France, and he seen and heard other Indians, like Choctaw, Comanches sending messages on the radio, on the telephone. Not coded, just talking their language. So, after he got discharged, his parents were already living here. So when he got discharged, he went to school in LA, graduated as an engineer. When he got back from work one evening, he was looking at a newspaper where he seen they were having maneuvers in Louisiana where some of those Indians were trying to send messages. And then he saw right away that he should demonstrate how to put a code in Navajo. And then the following day, he knew that other Indians tried but it wasn't in code. And they sent Germans and Japanese here to study these other languages, but not the Navajo. So he went to Camp Elliot, to General Vogel, and then he explained how he wanted to demonstrate how to set up a code and then General Vogel said that this has been done before. It won't work. Anyway they gave him permission to do that. So he went, back to LA to the employment office where he picked up well-educated Navajos, about six of them. At least he got five from employment office. The sixth one was Navy person; we don't know who that Navy person was. He was a new recruit at San Diego Naval Training Station. So they gave him two weeks to try it, to send messages, use certain words to spell it out, so they made up a code. This wasn't in training—this was just a demonstration for the general and his staff to know how the code would work. So they give him eight messages. These were all spelled out and they came out okay (during the test). And then a couple weeks later, General Vogel gave permission to recruit at least two hundred Navajos, but before that there were only thirty, as a special project for the test. So this thirty—the recruiters here on the reservation—they got thirty recruits, and then this thirty, they took off from Gallup—between Window Rock and San Diego, they lost one. They still don't know who that thirtieth man was. They ended up with twenty-nine down there. Somebody dropped off on the way.

Q:    Somebody got lost along the way.

HF:    None of the first twenty-nine knew who the thirtieth man was. Different persons, when you mention this, they will say, "I was the thirtieth man, I was the thirtieth man." Stuff like that.

Q:    So we have several thirtieth men, right?

HF:    After the project—they went through boot camp like the other recruits—six weeks at the San Diego doing their duties. After graduation there, they went to Camp Elliot. And then it was really closed in project. It was a top, top secret. They would have bars on the windows and doors. And on the outside they got guards. And then they go back to the barracks. The first twenty-nine are the ones—just like a round table discussion, they sat there and each one of them say what the alphabet should use—name of animals here on the reservation. Like for instance, an A. You go outside, you see an ant. That's the first letter of the animals that you use for alphabet.

Q:    Then you use the Navajo word for ant?

HF:    Yup. For instance when they say (Navajo word)—it's "ant" in Navajo—you put the letter A. So B you say *shush*— that means "bear." And for C (Navajo word)—that means "cat." First letter of the animal. And then they went along and figure out, like *attack*—what do we do for *attack* or *charge? Advance?* And then *machine gun?* We don't have words in Navajo for that, but what do machine guns do? Rapid fire. So they said (Navajo word). So when you hear that, you put machine gun. And then for tank. What does a tank do? Crawl. So tank and turtle are the same thing in the code. And hand grenade. (Navajo word). Hand grenade is like a potato. And then for bomb (Navajo word), which means "blow up." The first twenty-nine set all that up. They give to you in the classroom. We had to check these things out, these files, and then check them back in, and at eight o'clock, we checked them out. We studied them until the break—we had a break, during the break you don't go outside. You stay around. You have your folder with you all the time. First thing that they said is that this is a confidential, top secret. Don't reveal this. After you go outside, don't say anything about this. If you're married, you don't say anything to your wife. If you're not married, if you have a girlfriend, hell no. Your brother, your father, your mother, your sister—nobody. This is a top, top secret. See we didn't know that. When we'd go on liberty—most of the men would go to Los Angeles. On Fourth Street, all the different tribes congregate there, come together there. Here on the rez, they don't have bars, but there it's open, so they go there. After they leave, after they go back to camp, the FBI goes in there and pick up these girls or whoever they were with to see if anything was revealed. If you do, out you go—transfer you to infantry. And they stressed that your pronunciation has got to be perfect. Your writing—you got to print, you can't use script. Just like being in the first grade again, you learn how to print again. They want it fast and clear. So that's the eight weeks we were in there. The first six weeks were classroom; the last two weeks were out in the field.

Q:      Practicing?

HF:     Practicing, training. We were even sent down to San Diego aboard the submarine. It would take us out to Catalina Island, a couple miles out, the submarine pull up, and then we take the rubber raft and then we hit the island and send messages back to the mainland. Then we did the final code. At Camp Pendleton, there's a landing area there so we'd land. So this is one of the field training that we had. The officer would give a person a message and then he'll sneak and go to another radio and see if that message comes out the same way. So that's the training we had.

Q:      Pretty extensive.

HF:     I never thought I was going to be as a code talker. I thought I'd be like any other Marine. And then after our eight weeks is up, then we shipped overseas—284 was my draft number. We were aboard ship fourteen days.

Q:      Where did you land?

HF:     At that time, Guadalcanal was secured. So we landed there. Then we were separated. Some when to First Marine Division; I was sent to Second Marine Division—headquarters signal company—Third Battalion, Twenty-Eighth Marines, Second Marine Division. And then Second Marine Division had hit Tarawa already. So we just went to the next island. It's adjacent to the channel and other islands next to Tarawa.

Q:      So when was the first time you had to apply all this training?

HF:     When we landed, we were going so fast we didn't have to transmit anything - until we secured the island. And then after that I was transferred to the Fifth Marine Division as it was forming, so they needed the code talkers. See, we're placed wherever we're needed.

Q:      How many different units of code talkers were there?

HF:     It's hard to say how many—like in Fifth Marine Division itself, we had thirty-eight of us, up from the division all the way up to the Admiral Nimitz (ship) all the way down to command ship, all the way down to battalion. See, I was with the battalion on frontlines.

Q:      How many code talkers in a division?

HF:     So, thirty-eight within the Fifth Marine Division. I think there were more than that or less than that in the Fourth

Marine Division. And then Third Marine Division was like that too, so in each division there's some. Something like a pool, wherever you're needed, they'll transfer you there.

Q:     You say thirty-eight, you mean thirty-eight different guys?

HF:    Yeah, thirty-eight different personnel.

Q:     When did you get out?

HF:    After the war, after Iwo Jima, we went back to Hawaii, and then we were getting ready to go to Okinawa again, which was the last island. We were supposed to be—the Fifth Marine Division was supposed to be—in reserve, but they didn't use us so after that, Nagasaki was bombed with the atomic bomb, so right after that, after Okinawa, the war was over. Then I spent four months at Nagasaki and four months at (a Japanese location)—occupation force. And then after that, I had enough points to come home, but I decided to go there to see what kind of a people, what kind of country it is.

Q:     Japan?

HF:    Yes, Japan.

Q:     Did you fight anymore?

HF:    No, not after—for me, not after Iwo Jima, it was a nothing after.

Q:     What did you discover about those people?

HF:    It's, it's something like us, but the center part of it- it's not so good. It's so darn crowded, after the occupation. There were just the policemen, are the only ones that, at each street corner—there's no civilians, no nothing. Then after that, they started coming—migrating back from the mountains back to the city.

Q:     So when you got back from there, you still couldn't talk about it.

HF:    No, I couldn't. It's so horrible to talk about it. It's after you go through your ceremony after the war—my parents told us not to talk about it anymore after that. So that was it, nobody talked about it.

Q:     Did the military keep it a secret?

HF:    It's not a secret. See, our code was declassified in 1956. It was declassified. And here they said they had code talkers in Europe and elsewhere, not even the Philippines; they didn't have any in the Philippines and none in Europe. Only in the Marines in the Pacific.

Q:     So after the purification ceremony, traditionally you didn't talk about your wartime experiences?

HF:    That's the way it was with me.

Q:     Some other tribes, they come back from battle and recount the deeds in battle, because that had something to do with becoming a chief or something. But that's not the tradition in Navajo?

HF:    No, we don't. It's just like a rank. See, after I got discharged, I was in the active reserve for fifteen years. When I got discharged, I had the rank of a tech sergeant when I got discharged, fifteen years after the war.

Q:     You kept that rank?

HF:    Yeah, active reserve.

Q:     Do you feel like there's anything else about your experience or the code talkers' experience in the military you'd like to discuss?

HF:    Each code talker's got their own experience. Like, Iwo— we went forward, up to observation to set up the forward command post. And then they start shelling. All our officers, all our sergeants, it was bombed. So our sergeant a day before asked me, he said, "Chief, since you're the senior on this squad of your original Fifth Marine Division, something tells me I won't be around the next couple of days." This was a code that he made—he said, "Chief, I want you to be in charge. You're the person that can take orders and give orders. You're that type of person." So I took charge, that's the way I am. That's where I got my field stripes. It wasn't on my record until later, fifteen years later.

Q: How come it took so long?

HF: I don't know. It's like—see all the veterans here, especially the code talkers, if they're given the Bronze Star and a citation, any kind of citation, they weren't awarded that. It's all mostly on paper. It's been fifty years now.

Q: So what other citations were you supposed to get?

HF: Unit Citation, Presidential Citation, National Defense, Asiatic with two stars, Victory Medal, two Purple Hearts with gold star because I was wounded twice.

Q: You were wounded twice?

HF: Yeah, Iwo Jima—enough to be evacuated. So, totally I got thirteen citations, which I never got. None of these. Fifth Marine Division never gave out awards. The Second Marine Division never gave out awards either. It's on their discharge papers. That's on paper.

Q: You mentioned earlier, and I want to get it on tape, so I don't miss it. This September you're going to Oklahoma with a group of code talkers.

HF: There's a lady—she's a Navajo living in Norman, Oklahoma. She's working at the University of Oklahoma. Her name is Effie Tsosee Tee. Tee is her last name. And she's from Klagetoh, Arizona, which is about thirty miles from here. She called me at my house and said that we'd like to have

Navajo code talkers come to Oklahoma in September. I asked her why. She said that the month of September is American Indian month (in Oklahoma). And then they're having the code talkers of the Comanche, the Choctaw, and would like to invite Navajo code talkers. So on the twenty-sixth and twenty-seventh they're having a powwow. See, I dance at the powwow. I dance the gourd dance in the powwow. So I'll be dancing with the Comanches.

Q:      This will be a unique event.

HF:     So after she gave me that I said, "How can we get the code talkers, that many?" She asked me how many code talkers there are. I said "Thirty-five." We got almost sixty, since 1971, that are registered with us, with the Navajo Code Talker Association, but only thirty-five paid their yearly dues, that come to the meetings. So I told her that we were having a meeting, and then I brought this up at that meeting and they said okay. So that part of it was the association saying, "Okay, we'll go there." So we'll meet with the Comanche code talkers, and in the mean time I called the Navajo transit office, that is to make arrangements to get the tribal bus to take us.

Q:      So you'll take a bus over there.

HF:     Bus load, yeah, with their, with their spouses. I think there'll be about twenty-three or twenty-four code talkers go.

HF:     I got her phone number at home. I can give you that so you can contact her. I'd like to meet those code talkers, even though they just talked in everyday language. It wasn't really a code. Ours was in code.

Q:      Are you involved in the discussions about a national Indian vet cemetery?

HF:     The code talkers are involved because we're the only organization that's got officers, and we're chartered in New

Mexico. The reason why we're in New Mexico is because we don't have an office or facilities where we can meet here in Window Rock on the Navajo reservation. We tried that. We asked for land or office space, but they never gave it to us, no. So the chamber of commerce in Gallup was good enough to say we can use their office, free. I'll make a contract. How many years you want to use that office? The room that we use used to be called Kiva, but they changed it to Navajo Code Talker Room.

Q:      So what's your title in the association?

HF:     I'm the vice president.

Q:      Thank you for your time, Mr. Foster.

# CHAPTER SEVEN

# The Preservation of American Indian Languages and Cultures

*J. P. Harrington (seated left) works with several American Indian "informants" to record the songs and speech patterns of California Indian peoples.*

```
sack  čɨlɨ, meš                savory, to be  tuštom
x̣ɨkm                          saw, to  aqlɨlɨ-wɨy
sacrum  ʔiko                   say, to  axutiwil, ʔip
sad, to be  šaqnikulš,         scabby, to be  puqpuqeč
   šu-mišup, takululun         scale (of fish)  yep
sage  wewey                    scar  akučuwič
sage, thistle (chia sp.) pax   scarce, to be  uqti-yɨw
salamander  tiqweneqwen        scare, to  saɨ-ulkuwin,
saliva  uqčɨk                      s-utaxtaxsɨn
salmon  ʔokowoč ~ ʔokowoyoč    scattered, to be  pilisa-nan,
salt  tip                          util-pakas, util-pamay,
saltgrass  liton                   wekey
```

*This is a sample page of a linguist's notes demonstrating the use of phonetic spellings when indicating the pronunciation of a language.*

And so the question must be asked: what might have been the ultimate cost to America and her freedom if the alternating federal policies of genocide and assimilation had been successful with regard to American Indians and their languages?

From the onset of the European invasion of the Americas that started in 1492, foreign Christian political powers consistently failed to recognize or value American Indian cultures, naming them the products of the minds of "savages" in official state policies and even the products of the devil in some church proclamations.

In more recent times, citizens of the United States, and the world for that matter, have begun to mature in their attitudes toward indigenous peoples, their languages, and their cultures. One could say there has been considerable progress.

The US federal government, in the 1960s and 1970s, at long last arrived at the policy of self-determination with regard to American Indian tribes and began methodically transferring the responsibility for making decisions and operating programs that affected the lives of American Indian people to tribal governments.

In 1990 the United States Congress even passed the Native American Languages Act, which recognized the unique status of American Indian languages and cultures and called for the means to ensure their survival. The law, also known as Public Law 101-477, declared that from that time forward it was to be the policy of the United States to preserve, protect, and promote the rights and freedoms of American Indians to use, practice, and develop their languages. The entire text of the law is included here because it reflects the policy that should be in place in all nations regarding the treatment of indigenous languages and because it reflects such a stark reversal of the US government's policies toward native languages. (Again the author is quoting this legislation verbatim, which includes the term *Native American* instead of *American Indian*.)

## PUBLIC LAW 101-477; NATIVE AMERICAN LANGUAGES ACT

### SHORT TITLE

SEC. 101. This title may be cited as the "Native American Languages Act."

## FINDINGS

SEC. 102. The Congress finds that-

(1) the status of the cultures and languages of Native Americans is unique and the United States has the responsibility to act together with Native Americans to ensure the survival of these unique cultures and languages;

(2) special status is accorded Native Americans in the United States, a status that recognizes distinct cultural and political rights, including the right to continue separate identities;

(3) the traditional languages of Native Americans are an integral part of their cultures and identities and form the basic medium for the transmission, and thus survival, of Native American cultures, literatures, histories, religions, political institutions, and values;

(4) there is a widespread practice of treating Native American languages as if they were anachronisms;

(5) there is a lack of clear, comprehensive, and consistent federal policy on treatment of Native American languages which has often resulted in acts of suppression and extermination of Native American languages and cultures;

(6) there is convincing evidence that student achievement and performance, community and school pride, and educational opportunity is clearly and directly tied to respect for, and support of, the first language of a child or student;

(7) it is clearly in the interests of the United States, individual states, and territories to encourage the full academic and human potential achievements of all students and citizens and to take steps to realize these ends;

(8) acts of suppression and extermination directed at Native American languages and cultures are in conflict with the United States policy of self-determination for Native Americans;

(9) languages are the means of communication for the full range of human experiences and are critical to the survival of cultural and political integrity of any people; and

(10) language provides a direct and powerful means of promoting international communication by people who share languages.

## DEFINITIONS

SEC. 103. For purposes of this title-

(1) The term "Native American" means an Indian, Native Hawaiian, or Native American Pacific Islander.

(2) The term "Indian" has the meaning given to such term under section 5351(4) of the Indian Education Act of 1988 (25 USC 2651(4)).

(3) The term "Native Hawaiian" has the meaning given such term by section 4009 of Public Law 100-297 (20 USC 4909).

(4) The term "Native American Pacific Islander" means any descendent of the aboriginal people of any island of the Pacific Ocean that is a territory or possession of the United States.

(5) The terms "Indian tribe" and "tribal organization" have the respective meanings given each of such terms under section 4 of the Indian Self-Determination and Education Assistance Act (25 USC 450b).

(6) The term "Native American language" means the historical, traditional languages spoken by Native Americans.

(7) The term "traditional leaders" includes Native Americans who have special expertise in Native American cultures and Native American languages.

(8) The term "Indian reservation" has the same meaning given to the term "reservation" under section 3 of the Indian Financing Act of 1974 (25 USC 1452).

## DECLARATION OF POLICY

SEC. 104. It is the policy of the United States to-

(1) preserve, protect, and promote the rights and freedom of Native Americans to use, practice, and develop Native American languages;

(2) allow exceptions to teacher certification requirements for federal programs, and programs funded in whole or in part by the federal government, for instruction in Native American languages when such teacher certification requirements hinder the employment of qualified teachers who teach in Native American languages, and to encourage state and territorial governments to make similar exceptions;

(3) encourage and support the use of Native American languages as a medium of instruction in order to encourage and support;

    (A) Native American language survival,

    (B) educational opportunity,

    (C) increased student success and performance,

    (D) increased student awareness and knowledge of their culture and history, and

    (E) increased student and community pride;

(4) encourage state and location education programs to work with Native American parents, educators, Indian tribes, and other Native American government bodies in the implementation of programs to put this policy into effect;

(5) recognize the right of Indian tribes and other Native American governing bodies to use the Native American languages as a medium of instruction in all schools funded by the Secretary of the Interior;

(6) fully recognize the inherent right of Indian tribes and other Native American governing bodies, states, territories, and possessions of the United States to take action on, and give official status to, their Native American languages for the purpose of conducting their own business;

(7) supporting the granting of comparable proficiency achieved through course work in a Native American language the same academic credit as comparable proficiency achieved through course work in a foreign language, with recognition of such Native American language proficiency by institutions of higher education as fulfilling foreign language entrance of degree requirements; and

(8) encourage all institutions of elementary, secondary and hirer education, where appropriate, to include Native American languages in the curriculum in the same manner as foreign languages and to grant proficiency in Native American languages the same full academic credits as proficiency in foreign languages.

## NO RESTRICTIONS

SEC. 105. The right of Native Americans to express themselves through the use of Native American languages shall not be restricted in any public proceeding, including publicly supported education programs.

## EVALUATIONS

SEC. 106. (a) The President shall direct the heads of various federal departments, agencies, and instrumentalities to-

(1) evaluate their policies and procedures in consultation with Indian tribes and other Native American governing bodies as well as traditional leaders and educators in order to determine and implement changes needed to bring the policies and procedures into compliance with the provisions of this title;

(2) give the greatest effect possible in making such evaluations, absent a clear specific federal statutory requirement to the contrary, to the policies and procedures which will give the broadest effect to the provisions of this title; and

(3) evaluate the laws which they administer and make recommendations to the President on amendments needed to bring such laws into compliance with the provisions of this title.

(b) by no later than the date that is 1 year after the date of enactment of this title, the President shall submit to Congress a report containing recommendations for amendments to federal laws that are needed to being such laws into compliance with the provisions of this title.

## USE OF ENGLISH

SEC. 107. Nothing in this title shall be construed as precluding the use of federal funds to teach English to Native Americans.

*Approved October 30, 1990.*

On an international scale, in the 1990s the United Nations began developing an official international policy on the rights of indigenous peoples. For more than ten years, the international community debated this issue. Finally, in 2007, that declaration, known as the United Nations Declaration of the Rights of Indigenous Peoples, was finally ratified with 143 nations in favor and four against. The opposition votes were cast by Canada, Australia, New Zealand and, somewhat surprisingly, the United States. It wasn't until 2010 that the United States reversed its position on the issue and ratified the UN declaration, as did the other three hold-out nations.

Article XIII of the declaration states that indigenous peoples
have the right to revitalize, use, develop, and transmit to future
generations their histories, languages, oral traditions, philosophies,
writing systems, and literatures, and to designate and retain their
own names for communities, places, and persons.

Article XIV of the declaration states that indigenous peoples
have the right to establish and control their educational systems and
institutions providing educational systems and institutions in their
own languages, in a manner appropriate to their cultural methods
of teaching and learning.

The changes in policies within the US government and the United
Nations reveal that hopefully, finally, majority populations realize
that promotion of the languages and cultures of indigenous peoples
isn't only healthy for those indigenous peoples but for society as a
whole. As declared in the Navajo Nation's education department
documents in 1994, "Our work with the language has not been work
just on language in isolation. It has been part of a far larger effort to
restore personal and social wellness."

This is echoed in the language policy enacted by the tribal council
of the Pascua Yaqui Tribe several years ago: "Our language is the
foundation of our cultural and spiritual heritage."

So, together, may all Americans everywhere offer up our gratitude
and appreciation to American Indians for tenaciously holding on to
their indigenous languages and specifically to the American Indian
soldiers of World War I and World War II who used their native
words as weapons of war on our behalf in the ultimate language of
victory.

# Credits and Acknowledgments

The code talker interviews conducted in Norman, Oklahoma, in September, 1992:

Producer and interview questions by Gary Robinson
Interviewer: Kathryn Bell
Videographer: Scott Swearingen

Interview with Navajo code talker Harold Foster conducted at Window Rock, Arizona, 1992:

Interviewer: Gary Robinson

Special thanks to:

Comanche Nation Museum
Comanche Nation public information office
Comanche veteran Lanny Aseperme

Choctaw Nation public information office
Choctaw Nation office of the principal chief

Don Loudner, national commander, National American Indian Veterans

US Mint

Navajo Code Talkers Association

# Bibliography and Sources of
# Information for Further Reading

Allen, Phillip. "Choctaw Indian Code Talkers of World War I." *Choctaw Nation website.* http://www.choctawnation.com

Bloor, Colonel A. W. "Transmitting Messages in Choctaw." *U.S. Army Memo to Commanding General of the Thirty-Sixth Division*, Jan. 23, 1919.

Flaherty, Thomas H. and Henry Woodhead, eds. *The American Indians: The Way of the Warrior.* Alexandria, Virginia: Time-Life Books, 1994.

Imon, Frances. *Smoke Signals from Indian Territory, Volume II.* Wolfe City, Texas: Henington Publishing Company, 1977.

Hirschfelder, Arlene and Kreipe de Montano, Martha. *The Native American Almanac: A Portrait of Native Americans Today.* New York: Prentice Hall General Reference, 1993.

Britten, Thomas A. *American Indians in World War I.* Albuquerque, New Mexico: University of New Mexico Press, 1997.

Bernstein, Alison R. *American Indians and World War II.* Norman, Oklahoma: University of Oklahoma Press, 1991.

Daily, Robert. *The Code Talkers: American Indians in World War II.* New York: Franklin Watts, 1995.

Durrett, Deanne. *Unsung Heroes of World War II: The Story of the Navajo Code Talkers.* New York: Facts on File, 1998.

Hunter, Sara Hoagland. *The Unbreakable Code.* Flagstaff, Arizona: Northland Publishing, 1996.

Littlefield, Holly. *Children of the Indian Boarding Schools.* Minneapolis, Minnesota: Lerner Publishing Group, 2001.

Meadows, William C. *The Comanche Code Talkers of World War II.* Austin, Texas: University of Texas Press, 2002.

Plunkett, Barry. "Oklahoma's Greatest War Hero Also Choctaw Code Talker." *The Valliant Leader,* Sept. 9, 1987.

Pyle, Chief Gregory E. *Official State of the Choctaw Nation Address,* Sept. 6, 1999.

Rebecca Robbins Raines. *Getting the Message Through: A Branch History of the US Army Signal Corps.* Washington, DC: US Army Center of Military History, 1996.

Schupman, Edwin. "Native Words, Native Warriors." *Museum of the American Indian website.* Washington, DC. http://americanindians.si.edu/education/codetalkers/html/index.html.

Seelinger, Matthew J. "124th Signal Battalion." *The Army Historical Foundation*, Washington, DC. http://www.armyhistory.org/ahf2.aspx?pgID=877&id=332&exCompID=56

Unknown author."Code Talkers Suggested by Choctaw Soldier." BISHINIK (Choctaw Nation newspaper), Sept. 1986.

Look for the companion *The Language of Victory* DVD, which features never-before-seen interviews with Choctaw, Comanche, and Navajo code talkers of World War II. Available online from www.naivonline.com.

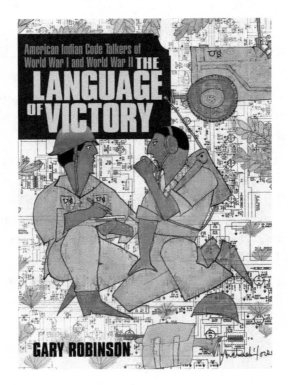

A portion of sales of *The Language of Victory* book and DVD goes to National American Indian Veterans (NAIV) to support programs and services benefitting American Indian veterans.

CPSIA information can be obtained
at www.ICGtesting.com
Printed in the USA
LVHW041500120619
621002LV00002B/405/P